OCCASIONAL PAPERS IN INTERNATIONAL AFFAIRS

Number 29

JANUARY 1972

Copyright © 1972 by the President and Fellows of Harvard College

Library of Congress Catalog Card Number 78–186335

ISBN 0–87674–024–7

Printed in the United States of America

Price $4.00

ABOUT THE AUTHOR

Eric A. Nordlinger received his Ph.D. from Princeton University in 1966 and spent 1968–1969 as a Fellow at the Center for International Affairs, Harvard University. Currently an Associate Professor at Brown University, he is continuing his research on conflict and conflict regulation while holding a Ford Faculty Fellowship in Political Science. He is the author of *The Working-Class Tories: Authority, Deference and Stable Democracy* (1967), editor and contributor to *Politics and Society: Studies in Comparative Political Sociology* (1970), and the writer of several articles on European and nonwestern politics which have appeared in *World Politics* and the *American Political Science Review*. He has just completed *Decentralizing the American City: A Study of Boston's Little City Halls* (1972).

As I was completing this study, the *New York Times* reported that with the killing of two British soldiers in Northern Ireland more than one hundred men, women, and children had been killed in this intense conflict between Protestants and Catholics. And there is reason to expect that the violence may become more extensive. The present study deals with such deeply divided societies, in which widespread violence, governmental repression, or both, are likely to occur. My goal is the development of a theoretical statement which can explain when, why, and how such intense conflicts are successfully regulated. By successful regulation I mean a condition marked by the absence of mass violence and forceful repression.

As I quickly learned, the task is not an easy one. I will mention only two reasons which make the delineation of an explanatory theory especially difficult. The relevant literature is limited and existing hypotheses are for a variety of reasons unacceptable. Yet the problem is of such great importance, the stakes are so high, there are so many deeply divided societies, that an attempt to account for the presence or absence of violence and repression hardly requires justification. Just as the odds do not favor the successful regulation of intense conflicts, the chances that a theory of conflict regulation will turn out to be valid are also on the low side. Indeed, it is partly the low odds of the former which reduce the probabilities of succeeding in the latter. Explaining unlikely, improbable, or seemingly impossible outcomes is however generally more challenging than accounting for regularities and likely outcomes.

I am indebted to many friends and colleagues who were

sufficiently interested in the first draft of this study to offer numerous suggestions and criticisms. Some of them were also good enough to offer the kind of encouragement and praise which was not only gratefully received, but most important in my decision to pursue the problem further in the coming years. My thanks to Lewis A. Coser, Harry Eckstein, Milton J. Esman, James Hardy, Donald Hindley, Donald L. Horowitz, Michael C. Hudson, Samuel P. Huntington, Val R. Lorwin, Richard Rose, Rodney Stiefbold, and Lois Wasserspring. I am especially grateful to Arend Lijphart whose work closely parallels the present study. For despite my criticisms of his related hypotheses, he was kind enough to provide an extensive commentary on the first draft. Finally, I want to thank Marina S. Finkelstein for acting as a superb editor, as evidenced by our many disagreements about both content and organization.

For financial assistance, I am grateful to Samuel P. Huntington who invited me to spend a year at the Center for International Affairs, Harvard University, and to the National Science Foundation (Grant Number 01–GS–2098).

ERIC A. NORDLINGER

Boston
November 1971

"In Ar-rchey Road," as we all know, "whin a marrid couple get to th' pint where 'tis impossible f'r thim to go on livin' together they go on livin' together." This Dooleyesque wisdom undoubtedly has lost some of its validity even for families on Ar-rchey Road. But it is still relevant for societies. The twentieth century bias against political divorce, that is, secession, is just about as strong as the nineteenth century bias against marital divorce. Where secession is possible, contemporary statesmen might do well to view it with greater tolerance. That is a problem in attitude. There is also, however, a problem in relevance. In many cases political divorce is not possible. In a sense, indeed, such divorce is possible not when people have been living together but only when they have, at most, been living alongside each other. When the Catholics and Protestants in Northern Ireland, Christians and Moslems in Lebanon, Malays and Chinese in Malaysia, Greeks and Turks in Cyprus, Sinhalese and Tamils in Ceylon, and rich and poor in most societies, can't go on living together, they go on living together. They have no choice. The only question is what will be the costs and benefits to each of continued and unavoidable cohabitation.

Eric Nordlinger's important and succinct study focuses precisely on this problem. If people who intensely hate each other have to live together, under what circumstances are they likely to live in relative peace and security and under what circumstances will they be at each other's throats? In attempting to answer this question, undoubtedly a large number of contemporary social scientists would direct their attention initially and primarily to processes of economic development and social mobilization. They would analyze the comparative levels and rates of change for the relevant social groups of urbanization, occupational status, literacy, education, and income. The underlying assumption would be that when rates of change are high and differences in levels are decreasing, conflict is more likely. Some analysts have even thought it possible to predict communal conflict by extrapolating into the future the trend lines in these various components of modernization. Certainly, during the past decade communal conflict, in contrast, for instance, to social revolution, has emerged as the dominant form of social strife in both modernizing and modern societies. There have been few societies on any continent which have been free of this phenomenon. And the evidence all suggests that its frequency and intensity are clearly increasing. Modernization involves social mobilization; social mobilization generates communal identity and communal interaction; communal conflict and violence are the inevitable result.

Professor Nordlinger is to be commended for taking a different tack. He does not employ this social mobilization approach. Nor does he take issue with it. He wisely places it to one side until the end of his analysis and instead focuses on social conflict in a divided society for what it truly is: a political problem. As a political problem, it can be exacerbated or moderated by the actions of political leaders and by the nature of the political institutions they create. Professor Nordlinger consequently devotes his energies to identifying the political methods and practices which appear to be effective means of regulating conflict in a divided society. He demonstrates convincingly that political methods, policies, attitudes, and organizations do make a decisive difference, and that the most significant influences on conflict regulation in a divided society are the skill and power of political leaders. Communal conflict and violence, then, are due not so much to the success of social-economic modernization as to the failure of political leadership. This is, in one sense, a highly optimistic conclusion but, in another sense, a very sobering one.

Professor Nordlinger thus approaches his problem in an essentially Madisonian spirit. Madison was concerned with identifying the political institutions and practices which would make republican government possible in an extensive society with many political factions and economic interests. Nordlinger is concerned with identifying the political institutions and practices which will make social peace possible in an open society deeply divided between two major communal or class groups. Like the authors of *The Federalist* he draws upon the evidence of a variety of historical cases to reach his conclusions. The result is a volume in which careful analysis has tightly bound together empirical data, scholarly generalization, and policy import. There is much thought in this brief study, and its argument and analysis deserve the attention of all those with a scholarly or practical interest in how social groups who hate each other can still go on living together.

SAMUEL P. HUNTINGTON

Member, Executive Committee of the Center

HARVARD UNIVERSITY
JANUARY 1972

TABLE OF CONTENTS

The "Relevance" of Conflict Regulation

This study deals with conflict regulation in deeply divided societies featuring open regimes. How and why are some intense conflicts regulated, while others lead to widespread violence, governmental repression, or both? Our concern falls squarely within what may be described as a conflict approach to the study of politics. This approach centers on several questions. How and why do conflicts arise? What are the various ways in which conflicts may be usefully classified? What are the typical kinds of strategies through which different types of conflicts are pursued? How are conflicts resolved, managed, or regulated? What impact do various types of conflict have upon society and the performance of governments? This is not the place to develop the questions, concepts, and hypotheses which inform the conflict approach. Nor is it therefore appropriate to delineate its particular strengths and weaknesses. But we can, in this introduction, underline the significance of one crucial dimension of the conflict approach which informs this study—that of conflict regulation.

"The crucial problem in politics is the management of conflict. No regime could endure which did not cope with this problem. All politics, all leadership and all organization involve the management of conflict." [1] Schattschneider's statement—though somewhat exaggerated—nevertheless contains an especially important point. If conflict management (or regulation) is empirically central to the functioning of political institutions, then it should serve as a major focus for the study of politics. Schatt-schneider's statement contains another important implication. Given the centrality of conflict management to most political phenomena, and assuming that the generalizations drawn from the present study enjoy a good measure of plausibility, they may with some advantage be applied to other problems and questions. This possibility deserves additional consideration.

In studying conflict regulation in deeply divided societies featuring democratic or, more broadly, open regimes, we are searching for the factors which account for the stability of such regimes under conditions of severe stress. If the study is read in this light, it may help also to correct certain imbalances in empirical democratic theory. The mainstream of the recent literature emphasizes attitudinal and socio-economic explanations at the expense of political ones, it is concerned almost entirely with the maintenance of democratic institutions rather than their emergence, and it deals primarily with clearly successful or unsuccessful democratic regimes while paying little attention to those that hang in the balance.

The present study contributes to the rectification of these imbalances both in its formulation of the problem and in its identification of explanatory variables. More important, this study may play some part in the development of a democratic model which will differ considerably from the one now widely accepted. The latter features social homogeneity, conflict within a wide consensus, moderate partisanship, crosscutting divisions, and social trust as virtually necessary conditions for the maintenance of democratic institutions.[2] But while applicable to many democratic regimes, such a model certainly does not correspond to all. Democratic regimes *are* found in deeply divided societies, even though communal divisions obviate social homogeneity, the conflict issues often leave only a narrow margin of consensus, emotion-charged beliefs entail a high level of partisanship, crosscutting divisions are rare, and deeply ingrained hostile and invidious attitudes toward members of opposing segments rule out feelings of social trust.

This skeletal statement contains two important implications for democratic theory. First, democracy is apparently possible without the conflict-mitigating influence of homogeneity, consensus, moderate partisanship, crosscutting divisions, and social trust. And second, since democracy is possible in the absence of these

[2]

conditions, then some other variables are presumably present which counteract the powerful centrifugal tendencies found in deeply divided societies. Taken together, these two points indicate the need for an additional democratic model.

Conflict regulation also clearly represents a major dimension of political integration. Some definitions of political integration explicitly define it as the absence of violence, most do so implicitly, and some definitions imply the absence of coercion, with governmental repression as the major variety. For Deutsch *et al.* political integration is present when different groups have formed a "security community," defined as a set of interrelationships "in which there is real assurance that the members of the community will not fight each other physically, but will settle their disputes in some other ways."[3] We could thus just as reasonably refer to our problem as the political integration of divided societies.

To restate hypotheses in different language often obfuscates rather than clarifies. On the other hand, doing so may draw attention to an overlap and thereby encourage the useful transference of hypotheses from one field of inquiry to another. The overlap between problems of political integration and conflict regulation is clearly brought out in a recent assessment of the integration literature, which identified its two major approaches as the "institutional-behavioral" (Deutsch) and the "conflict management" (Geertz).[4] Jackson and Stein went on to say that

> there is a failure on the part of the proponents of [the institutional-behavioral] approach to clarify the concept of conflict management and in particular to outline what kinds of responses are most likely to produce political cohesion in states exhibiting different patterns of conflict and disintegration. . . .The most important recent development in integration writings is the acknowledgement of the great and perhaps insuperable barriers to political integration, particularly in the newly independent states. The major factors impeding this process are the conflicts and divisions between different subgroups. . .within these states. These conflicts have intensified since independence and now seriously threaten the viability of many new nation-states. The conflict-management theorists approach political integration as a problem in defusing and moderating these conflicts so as to ensure a degree of consensus and stability in a society.[5]

In short, there is a distinct overlap between political integration and conflict regulation problems, so that studies of the latter may inform those of the former. But political integration studies usually do not give this overlap sufficient attention. The revision

[3]

of integration studies should continue so that the problem of conflict regulation may be accorded the extensive attention it deserves.

In the last few years there has been growing concern over what may be called "political performance": how well do regimes do what they are supposed to do—according to outside observers, participants, or both. American political scientists could probably arrive at a broad consensus on most performance criteria of regimes. The difficulties arise in explaining variations in regime performance. This is exactly what we shall be attempting here. In divided societies democratic (or open) regimes are faced with serious difficulties. To characterize them as stresses and strains would be a marked understatement. The regulation of intense conflicts, or the failure to do so, signifies how well or how poorly the regimes have performed in dealing with very real challenges, which could result in widespread violence, governmental repression, or both.

There is an additional reason for thinking that the present study gets at political performance. One regime's high performance on a particular dimension may be due to cultural, social, and economic factors beyond the control of elites and nonelites, whereas a second regime's equally high performance may be due to the purposeful efforts of elites, nonelites, or both. In terms of their absolute performance scores both regimes rate equally well. But in evaluating the two regimes we should award a higher score to the individuals in the second regime because it was through their purposeful efforts—requiring skill, effort, and perhaps sacrifice—that the regime achieved a high performance ranking. In the present study, it will be suggested that nonmanipulable cultural, social, and economic conditions may go a long way in accounting for the emergence of an intense conflict but, once it has become severe, its successful or unsuccessful regulation will be largely dependent upon the purposeful behavior of political elites. The regulation of intense conflicts therefore constitutes an extremely important and meaningful dimension of political performance.

Given the compartmentalization of the political science discipline, we sometimes forget that, if properly formulated, a proposition has two uses. If variable Y can explain variable X, the absence of Y should also help account for the absence of X. The dependent variable in this study is a nonviolent, though not

[4]

necessarily orderly, politics. Any plausible explanations which emerge should therefore also apply to this question: when and why do men engage in political violence? At the end of his critical review of the literature on *Violence and Social Change*, Bienen noted that he had not discussed that literature on democratic theory which asks—"why no violence in a particular system or under certain conditions?"[6] As Bienen recognized, he might well have done so in order to arrive at a better understanding of violent politics, except that his intention was to review a different body of literature. Just as these two questions—why violence and why no violence?—and their answers clearly complement each other, explanations offered for conflict-regulating outcomes in this study may also help account for different types of violence, including turmoil, race riots, communal terror, guerrilla activities, violent coups, revolution, and civil war.

Finally, a study of intense class and communal conflicts experienced by open regimes may also help explain the outcomes of other types of conflicts, such as urban Black-White confrontations, conflicts in closed regimes, international crises, and relatively intense labor-management disputes. If this were to be done, however, our hypotheses would require marked modifications and additions.

In short, the potential significance of the present study extends beyond the already fairly broad problem of conflict regulation in divided societies. There is a close, and sometimes intimate relationship, between this problem and several others of a more inclusive nature. The study's significance may also be broadened if the analysis indicates the general utility and importance of the conflict approach, and of the notion of conflict regulation in particular.

I

A STATEMENT OF THE PROBLEM

Some societies featuring open, nonrepressive regimes are so deeply divided that they are eminently prone to political violence, governmental repression, or both. Yet, some intense conflicts do not give rise to widespread bloodshed or forceful repression. The conflicts have in one way or another been regulated. This study's central goal is the development of some generalized statements which can explain the presence or absence of conflict-regulating outcomes. We are not asking how or why intense conflicts have emerged. Nor does the study deal with intense conflicts in closed regimes. Its theoretical universe is circumscribed by two criteria: existing intense conflicts and open regimes. A fuller investigation in which these restrictions are relaxed is to follow in a projected book-length study.

The problem must now be delineated in sharper form through the introduction of some essential definitions.

Definitions

All societies are differentiated along class lines, communal lines, or both. (Class divisions refer to objective group differences in wealth, income, and occupation. Communal divisions refer to ascriptive criteria, including racial, tribal, religious, linguistic, and ethnic differences.) At least one such socially differentiating characteristic is found in all societies. Individuals do not consistently

[6]

attribute a good deal of salience to social differences, subjective salience not varying uniformly with objective reality. However, when the two are found together—when a sizeable proportion of individuals who share some class or communal characteristic become subjectively aware of their similarity to other such individuals, value that similarity positively, and attribute some importance to it in defining their relations with individuals who do not share that social characteristic—then these social differences may be said to draw people into *segmental divisions* or *segments*.

If segments take on a high degree of political salience, as they invariably do in deeply divided societies, they will form the bases of *conflict groups*. Conflict groups develop when a significant number of individuals believe that their segment's social identity, cultural values, or material interests conflict with the segmental attachments of other individuals and are inspired to political efforts designed to influence the conflict's outcome.

These conflict groups, in turn, often give rise to *conflict organizations*, which are structured relationships among conflict group members devoted wholly or in part to the conflict with the opposing conflict group. Conflict organizations may include political parties, from small elite parties of notables to mass parties enjoying great organizational depth, paramilitary formations, trade unions, churches and religious orders, as well as a panoply of tribal, linguistic, racial, ethnic, and religious associations. Conflict groups and conflict organizations are by definition engaged in political conflict.

But not all political conflict is of interest here, since this study is limited to the outcome of *intense* or *severe* conflicts, or in other words, conflicts characteristic of *deeply divided societies*. Therefore, defining an "intense conflict" is crucial to the study. Not only does the term circumscribe the universe to which our theoretical statement is applicable, it has been defined in several ways and we must make our own meaning clear.

Eckstein, for example, defines intensity according to membership in conflict organizations,[1] or, in our terminology, the proportion of conflict group members belonging to a conflict organization: the higher the proportion of people directly involved in the political conflict, the greater its intensity. This definition would be especially easy to apply, simply requiring a tally of conflict organization members. However, it is not an especially appropriate definition because the extensiveness of

[7]

membership in conflict organizations may be used to help explain the regulation of "intense" conflicts. A possible independent variable should obviously not be used to define the universe of cases whose variations it is to explain.

Intensity might also be defined in terms of the distance separating opposing conflict group goals or of the incompatibility of their goals. Distance and incompatibility could be assessed by an outside observer or by the conflict group members themselves, but neither method can circumvent a crucial difficulty. A conflict may be "intense" even when the issue distance separating the conflict groups is relatively short and their goals are not incompatible. For conflict groups are often embroiled in "severe" conflicts because of deep-seated prejudices, long-standing jealousies, invidious beliefs, and emotionally-charged animosities which have little relationship to the distance and incompatibility of the issues themselves. When conflict group antagonisms are sufficiently powerful, a conflict over a seemingly easily reconcilable issue may become "severe."

A third possible definition, and one that is commonly found in the literature, assumes a close correspondence between the presence of two or more mutually reinforcing segmental divisions and the conflict's "intensity." When opposing segments or conflict groups not only divide on religious issues, for example, but on linguistic and economic ones as well, then it is commonly assumed that the conflict is "intense." There is, however, a problem, since the definition is founded upon a hypothesis whose validity has by no means been established. Despite the widespread acceptance of the crosscutting divisions hypothesis, it therefore cannot serve as a definition. Moreover, even if the statement that mutually reinforcing divisions almost invariably give rise to "intense" conflicts were accepted as valid, it could be that some conflicts limited to a single segmental difference are equally "severe."

A fourth definition is sometimes implicitly or explicitly suggested when it is assumed that subcultural divisions entail intense conflicts. When a society is divided into two or more subcultures there is very little interaction or communication between them; they differ markedly in their socio-economic characteristics, social values, or both; and each features an exclusive and extensive organizational network, ranging from political organizations to leisure-time associations. Such subcultural divisions are said to exist in present-day Austria, Belgium, and Holland. The problem

[8]

with such a definition is the absence of a sufficiently close association between a conflict's "intensity" and the extent of subcultural divisions. Although the great majority of "intense" conflicts are based upon such divisions, the latter do not regularly result in "intense" conflicts. There may be, and often is, a world of difference between even the most deeply and extensively segmented societies and those experiencing "intense" political conflicts.

A fifth definition has been suggested by Dahrendorf, the foremost contemporary conflict theorist. He conceives of intensity in terms of the "energy expenditure and degree of involvement of conflicting parties. A particular conflict may be said to be of high intensity if the cost of victory and defeat is high for the parties concerned." [2] The first part of the definition, energy expenditure, is too diffuse, vague, and undiscriminating, as well as being exceptionally difficult to measure. The second element, the costs entailed in victory or defeat, is a meaningful criterion which skirts the problems raised by the notions of issue distance and incompatibility of objectives. Issue distance and incompatibility may be prominent, but costs not necessarily be high. However, the notion of cost is perhaps too vague insofar as nothing is said about the kinds of costs and benefits.

Given these difficulties, a two-fold definition of our own is apparently warranted. A conflict is intense when the issues at stake are thought to be of the greatest importance, involving the segment's social identity, its most sought-after material rewards, its most cherished cultural values, or its perceived inalienable rights. An intense conflict is also present when at least one segment views another according to highly unflattering stereotypes, invidious beliefs, long-standing jealousies, and deep-seated prejudices, which, when taken singly or together, produce strongly felt and emotionally charged antagonisms. Although these two types of intense conflict are analytically and to some extent empirically distinct, the second type rarely occurs without giving rise to the first, and when the first is present over a sufficiently long period of time it is likely to engender the second. In short, a conflict is intense (or a society is deeply divided) when a large number of conflict group members attach overwhelming importance to the issues at stake, or manifest strongly held antagonistic beliefs and emotions toward the opposing segment, or both. It now becomes apparent that intense conflicts may readily result in widespread violence and repression when one conflict group controls the government or the army. It should now also be clear that very few, if any, intense conflicts are resolved in the short run; the most that can be expected is their regulation.*

As has been noted, the present theoretical statement is not intended to apply to all deeply divided societies; it is limited to those with open regimes. *Regimes are open* when power is relatively diffused between the elite and the nonelite. It will then usually be diffused within the elite itself, but this is not a defining criterion. Admittedly, this is a loose definition. However, in order to include regimes which are not fully democratic, I found it necessary to resort to a relatively unspecific one, rather than the more satisfactory type of procedural definition by which democratic regimes are usually defined. Yet the definition does have a singular advantage. When power is relatively diffused between the elite and nonelite we can go a long way toward predicting the presence of other characteristics which may be viewed as meaningful dimensions of a regime's openness. For one thing, a diffused power structure is likely to be found alongside associations which are both politically involved and autonomous from the government. We may also be confident that there are channels which allow for the expression of significant political demands of a substantive or procedural variety. Governmental decisions are significantly influenced by conflict, competition, and compromise among the various politically relevant associations. And there is a minimum of repressive law and "legal" violence. Coercion is usually directed only against individuals and groups who themselves rely upon the threat or use of force to alter the regime's structure, policies, or incumbents.

Regimes are usually neither completely open nor entirely closed. Developing a set of operational indicators and collecting the relevant data to measure a regime's openness is clearly beyond the scope of the present study. The most that can be done here is to set out those regime types which qualify as open. Democratic regimes, featuring universal suffrage, free elections, and genuine

---

* For the sake of brevity and style I shall sometimes refer to intense conflicts simply as conflicts and deeply divided societies as divided societies. When references are made to conflict regulation or regulatory outcomes they shall always mean successful outcomes. For the sake of brevity I shall also write as if deeply divided societies contain only two important conflict groups, although, unless noted differently, the generalizations are thought to be equally applicable to the few societies with three or more major conflict groups.

[10]

competition between two or more parties, clearly qualify as open regimes. Power is diffused between the elite and nonelite, and within the elite itself. Consequently, the other dimensions of a regime's openness are also present. Nineteenth-century Europe's semirepresentative oligarchies qualify as open regimes. The franchise was highly restricted, but the middle classes in these societies did enjoy a reasonable measure of power based upon their members and wealth. In contemporary terms practically all western regimes, as well as some nonwestern ones, such as Malaysia, Lebanon and India qualify as open. Other nonwestern regimes also qualified as open at particular times insofar as they had, for some reasonable period since independence, featured democratic characteristics. In fact, the transformation of some of these open regimes into closed regimes—as in the Sudan, Nigeria and Pakistan—constitutes a conflict-regulating failure.

Among contemporary nonwestern regimes more than half have experienced shorter or longer periods of military rule since independence. A significant proportion of these regimes may be characterized as open, although barely so. Among military regimes, those that are relatively open feature a return to civilian rule within a short time. While they are in power, the officer-politicians do not resort to repressive measures in order to maintain themselves in office, and political parties and other politically involved organizations are allowed to continue many of their activities. On the other side of the putative dividing line between open and closed regimes are found all colonial regimes, traditional monarchies, single-party regimes of the mobilization variety, communist states, and of course authoritarian and totalitarian regimes.

Given an intense conflict in an open regime, what would constitute its successful *regulation*? The question is easy to answer at the extremes. The absence of widespread violence and governmental repression constitutes a successful regulatory outcome. When there is no violence whatsoever and in the absence of repressive measures, conflict regulation has clearly succeeded. It has succeeded even if the conflict remains intense—few severe conflicts are resolved in the short run—and even if there are marches, demonstrations, expressive rioting, strikes, destruction of property, arson and looting. American political scientists are wont to be overly sensitive to such hostile and remonstrative acts, consequently labelling as violent many civil disorders in which no

[11]

lives are lost. Such disorders may more meaningfully be viewed as measures of the conflict's intensity rather than as indicators of a regulatory failure.

At the other extreme, conflict regulation has demonstrably failed when widespread violence occurs in the form of a civil war with a death toll running into many thousands, or when an open regime becomes closed as the dominant conflict group uses the "agencies of social control" to repress, imprison, or slaughter members of the opposing segment. It is more difficult to establish a threshold somewhere between these two extremes which meaningfully distinguishes between successful and unsuccessful conflict regulation.

In offering a few comments with regard to the identification of such a threshold the most that can be done here is to set out some rough guidelines for differentiating regulatory successes from failures. For example, should it be said that conflict regulation has failed when fifty to one hundred people are killed in a single riot or in a clash with police? Probably not. Riots *per se* are not indicators of failure, and whether any particular riot or demonstration produces one death or one hundred deaths is most often the result of accidental and thus unpredictable factors. Does it then make sense to move the threshold up to two hundred deaths in any one "instability event?" Again, the answer would seem to be "no." Given the conflict's intensity it is sometimes more sensible to be surprised (if not pleased) that *only* two hundred people lost their lives. In other words, the threshold should be sufficiently high to minimize disagreement as to what constitutes a regulatory failure.

Over and above the number of deaths, the time span during which the "instability events" take place also needs to be taken into account. A single riot in which one or two hundred people die does not denote a regulatory failure, but if such costly encounters recur over a period of years, then we certainly should label the experience a failure. It would thus seem appropriate to rely upon two thresholds. Conflict regulation has failed when three to four hundred people have lost their lives in any single "instability event." Regulation has also failed when more than one thousand people have died over a consecutive five-year period, as the result perhaps of a series of riots, sporadic outbreaks of terroristic violence, guerrilla clashes, a small-scale civil war, or any combination of these. Almost needless to say, when the time

[12]

comes to test the theory a continuum will replace the dual either-or threshold in order to apply the method of concomitant variation. We will not only want to explain the failure to regulate intense conflicts; it will also be important to account for the extent of such failures.

Determining a sensible threshold for the failure of conflict regulation through governmental repression is more problematic. One threshold which seems readymade for this purpose is that line which differentiates open from closed regimes. However, this is an overly facile response since we can at best differentiate only roughly between open and closed regimes at the continuum's center point. Part of the problem is due to the numerous ways in which a government controlled by one conflict group can repress its opponents. The best we can do here, at least without getting into an extended discussion of several cases of repression, is to say that regulation has failed when an open regime has been transformed into one that is not only closed, but is found toward the closed end of the continuum. To be somewhat more specific, regulation will have failed when one conflict group uses its control of the government, army, or police, at least to partially "eliminate" the opposing conflict group members or leaders, outlaw its conflict organizations, jail its leaders, or place other debilitating restrictions upon its nonviolent pursuit of the conflict.

Toward the Development of a Theoretical Statement

Having outlined the problem and set out some definitions, one other crucial point remains to be discussed: how is a theoretical explanation of conflict regulation to be developed? Given the scarcity of relevant and plausible hypotheses in the literature, as well as my own assessment of the utility of different theory-building strategies, I decided to try to generate plausible explanatory hypotheses through the systematic delineation of a coherent approach to the problem. My efforts are systematic in the sense that I begin at the beginning, or at least at what I consider to be a sensible starting point, and move on to confront one question after another as they are suggested by answers to preceding questions. And while the questions rarely, if ever, receive fully satisfactory answers, they at least offer some helpful implications for identifying the next question and some pointers as to where the answers might be found. I have also tried to make this theory-building strategy as coherent as possible. Obviously a number of variables will help account for conflict regulation, and they will "stand" at different levels of explanation. The independent variables should therefore be related to each other as well as to the dependent variable directly, forming a theory in the literal sense —a number of inter-related hypotheses "standing" at various levels of explanation.

I have not purposefully patterned the present study according to Smelser's "value-added" explanatory model of collective behavior, but there is a considerable overlap. In Smelser's theory each new determinant of collective behavior operates within the context of the previous determinant, concomitantly ruling out other behaviors.[3] His explanatory model, like my own, takes the form of a funnel. But while Smelser begins at its broad base, looking at the broad determinants of "structural conduciveness" to collective behavior, my own efforts begin at the tip of the funnel and work downwards and outwards. This kind of systematic attempt to generate a coherent theory might result in a statement that is "potentially fruitful," "suggestive for future research," and of some "heuristic value," even if many of the hypotheses turn out to be invalid. For insofar as these efforts constitute a sensible approach to the problem, they will identify some of the crucial questions and explanatory phenomena in a general manner, at least implying where the more specific explanatory variables are to be found.

In systematically generating this theoretical statement I shall be relying upon six societies which have successfully regulated their intense conflicts. These six cases—they are not treated extensively enough to call them case studies—are useful in inductively implying certain hypotheses, introducing some evidence to support other hypotheses, and illustrating various general points. A word of clarification is in order. Other writers interested in related problems have already dealt with some of these cases. However, they sometimes confuse, or at least they fail to distinguish between, a period of intense conflict during which regulation succeeded, and a later period of less than intense conflict when regulatory outcomes simply persisted. It needs to be stressed that I shall be dealing with these six cases only with respect to those periods when the conflict was at a high level of intensity and its powerful centrifugal impulses were regulated. Explanations for the latter may be quite different than explana-

[14]

tions for the maintenance of stable and nonrepressive regimes *after* the intense conflicts have been regulated.

An example of a study which purports to explain the regulation of intense conflict, when in actuality it is dealing with the maintenance of political order *after* the most pervasive and intense conflicts have been regulated, is found in an article entitled "Nonviolent Conflict Resolution in Democratic Systems: Switzerland." [4] The author claims to be explaining that society's success in regulating its intense religious and linguistic conflicts. Yet, the linguistic conflict never became intense, the intense religious conflict was regulated in the nineteenth century, and the article deals almost exclusively with contemporary Swiss social and political patterns. The most that is being explained is the *continuity* of conflict-regulating outcomes. Similarly, in Lijphart's study of Dutch politics, the conflict-regulating explanations refer almost exclusively to the post-1945 period, whereas the severe religious and class conflicts were regulated at the beginning of the twentieth century.[5] While it is possible that some of the same factors might help explain both the regulation of intense conflicts and the persistence of regulatory outcomes, this is by no means necessarily the case. At the very least, the two quite different dependent variables need to be distinguished. Not only are they different, but one is far more difficult to explain and achieve than the other.

One possible objection to the problem's general formulation here and the selection of cases in particular is that the intense conflicts are taken as givens and their general causes and context not considered. Is it not virtually impossible to generalize about the causes of conflict regulation without taking into account the economic, social, political, organizational and attitudinal variables which are closely related to the conflict's emergence and intensification? Is this not putting the cart before the horse? My reply to the latter question is "yes," but the former question receives a decidedly negative response. Certainly in a fullscale study of deeply divided societies the horse should come before the cart; inquiry into the intensification of conflicts should precede explanations of their regulation. But the present essay does not purport to be that fully developed study.

More important, the objection falls down for two reasons of substance. There is no *a priori* reason for believing that a phenomenon cannot be circumscribed and then explained without first analyzing its emergence. In principle, the two problems

[15]

are analytically and empirically distinct. Second, while they may not be distinct in practice, it must specifically be shown why and where the two problems are so inextricably connected that they cannot be treated separately. It has to be shown that a particular condition which explains the conflict's intensification is (1) present in some but not other deeply divided societies, (2) that its presence or absence affects the likelihood of regulatory outcomes, and (3) that the problem's formulation (or the writer's ignorance) prevents its inclusion among those variables which account for conflict regulation. While the first two conditions are satisfied with regard to some explanatory variables, the third (and crucial) condition is not satisfied. Indeed, it turns out that there is one variable in particular which helps account for both the intensification of conflict and the failure to achieve regulatory outcomes (See Chapter VI). This hypothesis could have been fully developed in the present study despite the formulation of the problem in such a way as to ignore the emergence of intense conflicts. Yet I thought it better to reserve its full development for a later study which will deal with both the emergence and regulation of intense conflicts, especially since its explanatory power is decidedly greater in accounting for the former. Finally, my exclusive concern with the outcomes of conflicts after they have become intense is justified by one writer's conclusion in reviewing several leading studies of communal conflict in non-western societies:

> Taken as a whole, [the volumes] reveal much about the boundaries between sections [i.e., segments] and the inescapable struggle for group power. Such an emphasis upon cleavage is an accurate image of the dissensus and discontinuity prevailing in these fundamentally divided societies. Yet for all their insight into the drama of conflict, these works. . .tell us more about cleavages than about links, more about conflict than about cooperation and reciprocity. . . .The complete picture requires somewhat greater attention to adjustment, interrelatedness, adaptation, and exchange.[6]

It might also be argued that this theoretical enterprise is implicitly biased from the outset because our six cases are all instances of successfully regulated conflicts. Even if a plausible explanatory variable is found in each of the six societies this finding might be discounted on the possibility that the variable is also present in societies which have not regulated their intense conflicts. However, this study is designed to generate rather than to test hypotheses, and this may be done without relying upon regulatory failures. Indeed, there is a good reason to rely only upon regulatory successes. Almost by definition, an intense conflict will result in violence or repression unless certain conditions prevail which prevent these outcomes. These conditions obviously cannot be easily identified in cases of regulatory failures where they are presumably absent; whatever these conditions may be, they are to be found more frequently and in sharper form in cases of successful conflict regulation. I should also add that a number of regulatory failures do find their way into the theoretical statement to support and illustrate some hypotheses.

The theory developed here is meant to apply to western and nonwestern regimes as well as to nineteenth-century and contemporary ones. The six cases include two nonwestern regimes and four European regimes dating from 1830 to the present. It may appear that the theory's scope—any open regime confronted with an intense conflict—is too encompassing and diverse to allow for the generation of useful hypotheses. Three kinds of results might be predicted: overly abstract generalizations which are untestable and perhaps banal, numerous narrow-guage hypotheses each applicable to only a few cases, or general and testable hypotheses followed by many exceptions, each one of which is "explained away" by special circumstances. Whether my theory is valid or invalid, it has at least escaped these three possible pitfalls. Moreover, the first attempt to generalize about a broad phenomenon should be devoted to the development of hypotheses applicable to all the cases, despite their diversity. Admittedly, this could turn out to be an overambitious and ultimately unsuccessful undertaking. On the other hand, it may turn out to be partly or largely successful. The only way to tell is to make the more ambitious attempt. And if explanations do vary according to geographical space and historical time there is no reason why separate hypotheses could not then be developed to deal with these variations or subtypes. One such hypothesis—applicable only to communal conflicts in societies just beginning to modernize—found its way into the theory. Indeed, even powerful and valid explanatory generalizations should later be refined in the form of subsidiary hypotheses applicable to particular subtypes to enhance their specificity, explanatory power, and validity.

There are also some positive advantages accruing from our

[17]

efforts to develop an inclusive theoretical statement. The great variation in space and time may help suggest explanatory variables that would not be readily apparent if the focus were limited to one type of regime or one type of intense conflict. Explanations for the regulation of intense class conflicts in nineteenth-century Europe may suggest similar or different explanations for the regulation of intense communal conflicts among contemporary non-western regimes. The "nation-building" problems (if not efforts) of some European regimes are comparable to contemporary non-western experiences. I would also point to some good reasons why political scientists should go back to historical cases, in this instance, nineteenth-century European ones. The inclusion of historical cases provides a larger universe within which to test hypotheses, especially when searching for a critical case study; they allow a longer period for analysis; they sometimes provide a more sizeable and better researched secondary literature; and it may just be that "history is too important (and I would add, too interesting) to be left to the historians."

I would not claim that the six cases are representative of our universe. They were selected according to two criteria: their variations in space and time, and the adequacy of the secondary literature. In one of these cases, Belgium, we shall be dealing with three distinct intense conflicts, whereas the other cases involve only one period of intense conflict. Belgium was faced with a severe church-state conflict from the time of its creation in 1830 to 1958; between 1880 and 1920 it experienced a sharp class conflict; and from the 1950s to the present, Belgium has been racked by a highly charged linguistic-territorial conflict between Flemings and Walloons. Between 1890 and 1917 the Netherlands lived through an intense church-state conflict involving Protestants, Catholics and secularists, and during this same period the class conflict reached its highest level of intensity. It should be noted that I have some reservations about the Dutch case; its religious and class conflicts may not have been sufficiently intense to qualify it as one of our cases. However, since the issue remains in doubt, and since it would be advantageous to include a possibly less than intense conflict in order to gauge the range of the theory's explanatory power, I decided to rely upon the Netherlands as one of the six cases. During the Second Austrian Republic, more specifically, from 1945 to 1965, deep class and religious divisions were superimposed one on the other, but with-

[18]

out repeating the violence and repression of the first Austrian Republic. In nineteenth-century Switzerland the religious-territorial conflict between Protestant and Catholic cantons gave rise to an intense conflict and a small civil war in which less than 200 men were killed. Lebanon has been experiencing a severe conflict between Christians and Moslems since it gained its independence from France in 1943. And in Malaysia, the Malays and Chinese have clashed over economic, religious, linguistic, symbolic and political issues since that country achieved its independence from Great Britain in 1957. Additional information about these six cases is presented in the following chapters as it becomes relevant to the theory's development.

In short, as it now stands, the theoretical enterprise suffers from some gaps, limitations, and definitional haziness. However, since it does not pretend to be more than a theoretical exploration, and since the problems do not significantly detract from such an effort, they may be temporarily set aside until the time comes to develop and test the theory more rigorously and extensively. On the other hand, the present study does enjoy those advantages accruing to any effort which seeks to delineate a theory in a systematic and coherent manner.

II

Six Conflict-Regulating Practices

Considering the scarcity of hypotheses bearing directly upon the problem of conflict regulation, the systematic development of an explanatory theory should begin at the beginning; more specifically, with that aspect of the problem which overlaps the dependent variable but is not identical with it. We may begin by asking a question that is primarily descriptive since it is largely limited to the dependent variable: when intense conflicts are regulated, how are they regulated? What are the various conflict-regulating practices worked out by opposing conflict groups when they succeed in regulating their conflicts? We define conflict-regulating practices as those decision-making procedures, political arrangements, and behavioral rules which are potentially capable of accommodating antagonistic groups to one another, thereby providing the framework within which severe conflicts are regulated.

Beginning with a survey of these common practices serves to put some empirical flesh on the theoretical problem by providing some information about a number of deeply divided societies that have regulated their conflicts. The survey also allows us to advance some generalizations regarding effective and ineffective conflict-regulating strategies. Most important, it provides a theoretical beachhead from which it is possible to proceed further and it points to the most useful strategy for so doing.

Two caveats are in order. It is certainly not being claimed that when one of the six conflict-regulating practices is implemented conflict-regulating outcomes will always follow. The great gap that may separate practice and outcome is underlined by events in Colombia and Ceylon. In both instances the opposing conflict group leaders managed to work out mutually acceptable practices in order to regulate the conflict. But the conflict group members refused to accept these arrangements, allowing massive violence to continue in Colombia (1947–1951) and touching off communal arson, atrocities, and violence in Ceylon (1957). (See Chapter V.) On the other hand, it will be suggested that when conflict regulation does succeed, one or more of the six practices are invariably employed. Second, in describing these typical practices, it is not claimed that what follows constitutes a classificatory scheme. It is only a descriptive list.

Six Conflict-Regulating Practices

One effective conflict-regulating practice is the *stable governing coalition* between political parties. Always involving the major conflict organizations, such coalitions are formed prior to elections with the avowed aim of conflict regulation. They usually continue for two or three electoral periods. Stable governing coalitions do not include the common governmental coalition found in multiparty regimes even if the same political parties enter into coalitions in two or more postelection periods. Such coalitions may indirectly contribute to conflict regulation, but in most cases they represent marriages of political convenience or necessity unrelated to the goal of regulating the intense conflict.

Malaysia serves as an excellent example here. Malays and Chinese(45 and 37 per cent of the population respectively) have been engaged in an intense conflict centering on linguistic, religious, symbolic, citizenship, educational and economic issues. In addition, the two segments continue to exhibit mutually hostile, envious, and contemptuous attitudes. Yet even before independence in 1957 the United Malays National Organization and the Malayan Chinese Association (with the Malayan Indian Congress as a mini-partner), established a joint consultative executive, the Alliance Party. The conflict group heads on this executive agreed to offer a common electoral slate prior to each national election, although the three political parties preserved their distinct organizational identities and power bases. They also worked out common positions on crucial racial and constitu-

[21]

tional issues which were dividing the country. This coalition arrangement was renewed in the 1959, 1964, and 1969 elections.

A second instance of a stable coalition is found in post-1945 Austria. The outcome of the Red-Black conflict in the First Republic had been a short civil war, followed by the introduction of a "corporatist" dictatorship. After 1945 the *Lager*, literally meaning armed military camps, had been transformed into political rather than paramilitary organizations. But one of the most striking phenomenon in postwar Austria was ". . .the persistence of Lagerdenken, the suspicion that the opponent. . .will bring about, given the chance, the conditions of civil war which destroyed the First Republic."[1] In resurrecting the Second Republic out of the shambles of the First, the leaders of the Socialists and of the People's Party agreed to form a coalition government before the 1945 election. And this despite the mutual hostility and distrust between the Catholics, who were often seen as fascistically inclined, and the Socialists, who were perceived as bolsheviks by many of their opponents. "The Grand Coalition . . .has been likened to an armed truce with inspection on the field."[2]

The coalition arrangements were renewed before each national election up to 1966. These included decisionmaking arrangements whereby the party leaders not only sat in the cabinet, but the crucial decisions were made outside the cabinet by a handful of top leaders constituting the coalition committee.[3] Unlike the Alliance in Malaysia, the two major Austrian parties did not contest elections as a single body, although the voters were aware that a coalition government would follow after the elections. By 1966 it had become apparent that the Red-Black conflict of the First Republic had been regulated; the bloodshed and repression of the 1930s would not be repeated, despite the still salient mutual suspicions. Only then did the party leaders deem it safe to discontinue their Grand Coalition.

A second conflict-regulating practice relies upon the *principle of proportionality*. It may be applied in several ways. For example, elective and appointive government positions may be distributed according to the proportionate population size of the segments or to their relative electoral strength. The principle may also be applied to the government's allocation of scarce resources (e.g., new schools) to the segments in accordance with their relative size. Proportionality has been defined in an encompassing

[22]

manner when contrasted to the majority principle of "winner take all": "the basic characteristic [of proportionality] is that all groups influence a decision in proportion to their numerical strength."[4] The principle serves as an effective conflict-regulating practice insofar as it reduces the degree and scope of competition for governmental power, administrative positions, and scarce resources; these are proportionately reserved for particular segments rather than being entirely up for grabs by anyone who can grab them.

The principle of proportionality has been extensively applied in Lebanon. Lebanon contains fourteen different religious sects, with the intense conflict taking place between the Muslim and Christian sects. According to Hudson, a seemingly minor hostile act could touch off massive violence.[5] According to the unwritten National Pact of 1943, the highest elective governmental offices are reserved for members of the largest segments. This formula, which is still in force today, calls for a Maronite Christian President of the Republic, a Sunni Muslim Prime Minister, a Shiite Muslim Speaker of the Chamber of Deputies, and a Greek Orthodox Deputy Speaker and Deputy Prime Minister. Cabinet portfolios are also carefully distributed among Christians and non-Christians, with some cabinet positions being reserved for particular sects.[6] Proportionality is also applied to civil service positions. According to one constitutional provision, the "communities will be equitably (i.e., proportionally) represented in government employment. . .in order to promote harmony and justice."[7] Proportionality is also written into the electoral law, each sect being alloted a fixed number of representatives in the Chamber of Deputies according to its relative population size. It is also applied within each constituency, the sectarian composition of the constituency determining the number of deputies representing each sect.

In each constituency the candidates belonging to one religious sect compete against each other, thereby taking much of the Christian-Muslim conflict out of the electoral arena. And there is some advantage accruing to those candidates who play down the appeal to their own segment and cooperate with a candidate of another segment. The upshot is electoral competition, but of a kind in which "no community acts in such a way as to maximize the number of its representatives at the expense of the other. Instead of communal strife, a tendency to develop communal

[23]

cooperation between the candidates [of different sects] has been established." [8]

To turn to another example, in the Belgium of the 1950s and 1960s—deeply divided between Flemish-speaking Flanders and French-speaking Wallonia—a near 50-50 form of proportionality has been extensively used as a conflict-regulating practice. According to one Belgian writer:

> The maintenance of a careful equilibrium between Flemings and Walloons has apparently become an essential when a government is formed (or even when a single minister has to be replaced), when a committee or group of whatever kind must be created, even when its task is not a public matter, and, indeed, for every important appointment. Since party politics cut across this division, the result is often such a complicated puzzle that refuge has to be sought in a 'package deal': the proper equilibrium. . .[is] possible only if a number of sometimes very heterogenous appointments are made at one and the same time.[9]

In 1971 one of these informal practices was added to the constitution. A new article stipulates that with the possible exception of the prime minister, the cabinet must comprise an equal number of Flemish- and French-speaking ministers. The same devotion to the principal of equality is also found in the Belgian government's allocation of resources. When railway lines have to be abandoned, when industrial development projects are sited and financed, when roads are built, the decisions are made on the basis of equality rather than of "rational" criteria specific to the particular decision.[10]

In the Second Austrian Republic the *Proporz* has also been applied to all civil service positions, to the diplomatic corps, and to practically all positions in the nationalized enterprises and government-controlled firms. Between 1945 and 1966 the *Proporz* was also applied to all governmental decisions involving social and economic issues, which were determined by the relative strengths of the two parties in the legislature.[11] In contrast to Austria, in which the proportional distribution is finely tuned to the number of each party's legislative seats and thus to its relative electoral support, the Lebanese rely upon an outdated census and the Belgians upon a 50-50 distribution, even though the Flemish segment is somewhat larger demographically and smaller electorally than the Wallonian segment.

A third conflict-regulating practice, *the mutual veto*, provides that governmental decisions cannot be taken unless they are

[24]

acceptable to all major conflict organizations. This veto may extend to government decisions as a whole or only to those which bear upon the conflict's central issues. Unlike John C. Calhoun's concurrent majority principle, which applied only to the legislature, the mutual veto can also apply to cabinets and extragovernmental groups of leaders, such as the Austrian coalition committee. Calhoun underscored the potential conflict-regulating effectiveness of the concurrent majority principle. Governments structured according to this principle cannot, he said, act in any sphere without the agreement of all major segments and, since governmental activities are essential, the segments find themselves strongly drawn to compromise.

> Impelled by the imperious necessity of preventing the suspension of the action of government, with the fatal consequences to which it would lead. . .each portion would regard the sacrifice it might have to make by yielding its peculiar interest to secure the common interest and safety of all, including its own, as nothing compared to the evils that would be inflicted on all, including its own, by pertinaciously adhering to a different line of action.[12]

Clearly Calhoun is claiming far too much for his concurrent majority principle, yet there is some measure of truth in the argument. Even if opposing leaders are not forced or "impelled" to compromise the conflict's central issues, there is reason to suppose that the mutual veto will contribute compromise on issues which do not stand at the heart of the conflict. It would therefore indirectly encourage compromise on the central issues insofar as opposing leaders build up some experience, confidence, and trust in dealing with each other on less central issues.

Calhoun's other argument also enjoys some validity. He pointed out that the necessity to compromise (an assumption deriving from his first point) prompts each conflict group to select as leaders men "whose wisdom, patriotism, and weight of character would command the confidence of the [opposing conflict group leaders], in contrast to leaders whose primary qualification is their identification with the narrowly defined interest of their supporters." [13] A third reason could be added for thinking that the mutual veto can be effective as a conflict-regulating practice. It may be especially effective in mitigating the fears and anxieties of the weaker segment or conflict group, thereby encouraging their disavowal of a violent politics.

The mutual veto was extensively and rigorously applied

from 1945 to 1966 during Austria's Grand Coalition. At the outset of each coalition government the leaders of the Socialist and People's Parties affirmed their acceptance of the unanimity rule on all policy issues: the cabinet could act only after the coalition committee had approved the proposed policy and within the committee both parties exercised a veto power.[14] In the Belgium of the early 1960s this qualified form of majoritarianism also began to take hold. "Increasingly, in parliament and other gatherings, a majority decision is not regarded as sufficiently representative when a tabulation of votes for and against shows them not to be equally divided between the two parts of the country — even when the issue at stake is not at all one of Fleming versus Walloon." [15] These informal practices were recently incorporated into the constitution. As of 1971, a concurrent majority is required on legislation involving relations between the linguistic-territorial segments: a simple majority of the Flemish- and French-speaking representatives in both houses and two-thirds of the total votes cast in each house. Which is to say that each conflict group has a veto over intersegmental legislation. And in Lebanon the mutual veto exists as a tacit understanding between Muslim and Christian leaders.[16]

A fourth conflict-regulating practice might be labelled *purposive depoliticization*: conflict group leaders agree not to involve the government in public policy areas which impinge upon the segments' values and interests. Sometimes, purposive depoliticization is taken one step further, with the conflict group leaders agreeing, whether explicitly or tacitly, not to raise segmental issues during election campaigns. This practice may obviously be especially effective in containing the conflict at a particular level of intensity, perhaps even helping to dampen it.

In Lebanon, the conflict group leaders have adhered to both types of purposive depoliticization. Given the conflict's severity and extensiveness, most governmental actions are likely to touch upon the religious segments' raw sensitivities. As a result, the governments have studiously refrained from taking on more than a bare minimum of governing responsibilities. The Lebanese regime was very much a "night watchman state" prior to 1959. Moreover, Lebanese politicians consider it taboo to bring up any issues involving the religious communities in public, especially in the middle of an election. Similarly, in Malaysia the elites have regulated the communal conflict according to what has been called an "avoidance model." Wherever possible, public discussion of conflict-laden communal issues is avoided. "The underlying fear is that any serious public discussion of such issues, even in controlled institutional settings, is more likely to raise inflammatory passions than to produce solutions or even meaningful habits of discourse." [18] As in Lebanon, for politicians to do otherwise is considered taboo.

Conflicts may of course also be regulated by *compromises* on the issues which divide the conflict groups. Compromise refers to the mutual adjustment of conflicting interests and values. Although the outcome does not usually elate either conflict group, neither is sufficiently unhappy to render the outcome unacceptable. Compromise may be limited to a single issue, it may involve mutual adjustment on two or more issues, or each party to the conflict may realize practically its entire objective with respect to some different issue.[19] This third possibility is the most common in severe conflicts which almost always involve two or more separate issues. If the conflict groups' preferences on each issue were compatible and transitive, then they might agree on a compromise solution for each issue. Incremental adjustments would define a "just," "natural," or "rational" intermediate point on a common preference scale. However, when the issues center on such questions as the official language or church-state relations, preferences are incompatible and intransitive. Thus, if compromise is to occur, it must take the form of the large-scale barter agreement often found in international negotiations, which brings together several issues and awards each conflict group most of what it wants on one or more of them. When single issues cannot be directly compromised, each conflict group "wins" one and "loses" another.[20]

This type of "package deal" compromise is exemplified in the Netherlands, which went through a period of especially intense conflict at the beginning of the twentieth century. This conflict was regulated by the "national compromise" of 1917, whereby the anticlerical Socialists obtained universal suffrage, the Protestants and Catholics gained state subsidies for religious schools equal to those given to public schools, and the decline in the Liberals' parliamentary representation was arrested through the introduction of election by proportional representation.[21]

Despite the severe conflict between Catholics and Liberals at

[27]

the inception of the Belgian state, they also managed to reach a compromise acceptable to both conflict groups. The Constitution of 1831 embodied a degree of religious freedom that was exceptionally liberal in the Europe of Metternich and Wellington; while the constitution did not separate church and state, there was to be no established church even though Protestants and Jews constituted only 1 per cent of the population. The state was to stand on a solidly secular foundation. In return, Catholics obtained assurances that the state would not interfere with their churches, schools, or social services. Moreover, the state was to subsidize the officers and houses of worship of all recognized religions (i.e., the Catholic religion). This was a curious compromise, which combined a state-subsidized clergy and a supposedly religiously neutral state.[22]

The religiously inspired school conflict has been plaguing the Belgians since 1831, with some half dozen different compromise agreements effectively regulating it for well over a century. The conflict was seemingly resolved through the 1958 School Pact — a compromise worked out between the Catholic and nonconfessional conflict organizations. In this pact, "the Catholics accepted the principle that where neither the communes nor the provinces (nor private initiative) organized nondenominational elementary or secondary schools, the national state should do so. The Socialists and Liberals accepted the principle that public subsidies should cover teachers' salaries for private (i.e., Catholic) schools." [23]

Compromise on practically all outstanding issues is clearly evidenced in Malaysia, where the Alliance leaders agreed to the following terms at the time of the coalition's formation: Malay was to become the single national language, although English and Chinese would be used liberally in government and the schools. Islam was to be the state religion, though the constitution provided for the extensive toleration of other religions. The symbolic position of Malaysian Head of State was to rotate among the dozen sultans who also head the provincial states. Constituency boundaries were drawn to favor the rural areas, thereby assuring the Malays of safe majorities in the Federal Parliament. They were also to enjoy a continued predominance in the civil service, the military, and the police, as well as certain economic and educational preferences. For their part, the Chinese were to achieve what few Overseas Chinese have ever dreamed of realizing in other Asian countries: all the Chinese born in the country were to become full and equal national citizens. The Chinese were also accorded full political participation and rights to office-holding, as well as religious freedom and the liberal use of Chinese. Moreover, the Chinese were assured of free participation in the economy; except for foreign-owned businesses, the Chinse own and manage practically the entire modern economy. This extensive set of trade-offs allowed Esman to characterize the Malaysian compromise as "an instance of a superb political bargain, an integrative solution which realized great benefits for all parties, in many cases more than the original participants had ever expected to achieve." [24]

The sixth and final conflict-regulating practice refers to the granting of *concessions* by one of the conflict groups, as opposed to compromise, which entails mutual concessions or adjustments. Concessions may be made by stronger, equally powerful, or weaker conflict groups. Concessions offered by weaker groups are not concessions at all; their relative weakness impells them to make such offers. Concessions offered by conflict groups which are about as powerful as their opponents are not usually effective in regulating intense conflicts. The conflict may even be further intensified when the opposing conflict group interprets the concession as a sign of weakness, thus heightening its confidence in complete victory, and leading to greater intransigence and pressure on its part.

Two major studies of revolution have a direct bearing on the last point. Brinton has emphasized that prior to the English, American, French, and Russian revolutions the government had made some real efforts at reform.[25] And, generalizing from his study of the French Revolution, Tocqueville made the point that revolutions occur when things are getting better rather than worse, and he applied this statement to concessions offered by governments to potential revolutionaries. "Generally speaking, the most perilous moment for a bad government occurs when it seeks to mend its ways. Only consummate statecraft can enable a king to save his throne when after a long spell of oppressive rule he sets out to improve the lot of his subjects." [26] This sixth conflict-regulating practice is therefore limited to instances in which the markedly stronger conflict group offers concessions to a weaker one.

The upshot of this restriction is a paucity of instances in

[29]

which this practice has been employed. In deeply divided societies the predominant conflict group is rarely willing to make seemingly uncalled-for concessions. Yet when this practice is applied it will presumably have a pronounced positive impact upon the conflict's regulation. The predominant conflict group's distinctly conciliatory behavior may mitigate the weaker one's antagonistic feelings and hostile beliefs. The conflict may also be regulated, given the weaker conflict group's readiness to accept the offer. Not only is it a relatively advantageous offer, a refusal could convince the predominant group that such an intransigent opposition can only be dealt with violently or forcefully.

One of the few instances in which this practice was employed illustrates its effectiveness in regulating severe conflicts. In the first half of the nineteenth century the Swiss Federation was fiercely divided. The seven Catholic cantons were adamantly attached to their religion and to the principle of cantonal sovereignty. The fifteen primarily Protestant cantons placed an extremely high value on the expulsion of the Jesuits and a centralized form of government. In 1847 conflict regulation very nearly failed when the Catholic cantons proclaimed their independence and a short civil war ensued. But even during the Sonderbund War, the Protestant cantons, with their clear-cut military preponderance, chose as their commander-in-chief a general who could be counted on to avoid unnecessary bloodshed. Fewer than 200 men were killed—a death toll that is lower than that of some present-day communal riots. Three months after the civil war ended, the clearly predominant Protestants offered the defeated Catholic cantons three major concessions. They were accorded full and equal representation on the commission which was to draft a new constitution. The constitution was to provide for a Council of States in which every canton had an equal vote, creating a privileged position for the small cantons that had just been defeated. And instead of relying upon their political and military preponderance to form a much desired unitary state, the Protestant Radicals wrote a federal constitution. These self-denying actions "contributed greatly to the pacification and conciliation of the opposing forces in the country. It was so successful that, no later than the following year [1849] citizens of the defeated cantons. . .declared that they would offer their services to the Bund and fight in its army at the slightest sign of a threat to Switzerland from the outside." [27] And this declara-

[30]

tion, representing the permanent *resolution* of the conflict, was made by citizens of cantons which had only a few years earlier enjoyed the sovereign right to raise their own armies and conclude military treaties with foreign states.

It might appear that one important conflict-regulating practice has not been included here. With its division of powers between central and local governments, *federalism* would seem to be especially appropriate in divided societies with territorially clustered segments. as in the case of many linguistically and tribally divided societies. Federalism may also facilitate conflict regulation by providing territorially-based segments with a greater measure of political security, compared to their position in unitary regimes, where they would have no autonomy *qua* segments. There are, however, a number of reasons for not including federalism in this list of conflict-regulating practices.

Federalism differs considerably from other conflict-regulating practices in that it may more aptly be described as the objective of certain conflict groups rather than as a process through which the conflict is regulated. Even the mutual veto, which comes closest to federalism in constituting a particular substantive objective, is usually conceived as a procedural arrangement rather than a particular allocation of authority. Second, federalism may appropriately and conveniently be treated as a substantive outcome resulting from one or another of the six conflict-regulating practices. Switzerland's extensive federal arrangements, for example, are a product of concessions to the minority Catholic cantons; and in present-day Belgium the mutual veto entails *de facto* federalism, given the Flemish and Walloon segments' geographical exclusiveness. In fact, one writer has described federalism as "an institutionalization of compromise relationships." [28]

Third, compared to the six conflict-regulating practices, federalism may actually contribute to a conflict's exacerbation and the failure of conflict regulation. In some deeply divided societies it is impossible to draw state boundaries without including a large number of individuals belonging to segments whose territorial base is elsewhere. Federalism thus allows or encourages the dominant segment in any one state to ignore or negate the demands of the minority segment. The possible consequences vary, but they may very well lead to the conflict's further exacerbation, as happened with an Ibo minority living in Northern

[31]

Nigeria. Moreover, the combination of territorially distinctive segments and federalism's grant of partial autonomy sometimes provides additional impetus to demands for greater autonomy; when the centrally-situated or centralist-oriented conflict group refuses these demands, secession and civil war may follow. (For some additional comments on this possibility, see Chapter VI.) Finally, because of these and other reasons, federalism has not been markedly effective as a conflict-regulating practice. According to one student of African federalism, those regimes which have succeeded in their "integration efforts" have not relied upon federal arrangements. And where federalism has been employed, as in "Nigeria, Mali, East Africa, Ethiopia, and the Congo Republic, the results have not been notable for their enduring qualities. Federal systems have remained operative for relatively brief periods of time, followed by fissure into separate, sovereign parts or movement towards unitary systems. Federalism has proved brittle." [29]

The six conflict-regulating practices listed above certainly do not represent an exhaustive list. For example, the list does not include reliance upon third parties as neutral arbitrators, mediators, or experts, whose recommendations regarding the conflict issues are more or less binding upon the conflict groups. However, the practices not included in the list are either rarely applied to the kinds of intense conflicts we are dealing with, are generally ineffective in regulating them, or easily subsumable under one or another of the six practices. Dahl's review of sharp subcultural conflicts in the Netherlands, Belgium, Austria, Norway and the United States at different historical periods provides some support for this point. "Conflicts involving subcultures are likely to be especially intense, and therefore particularly difficult to manage, because they cannot be confined to single, discrete issues; to the person sharing the perspective of a subculture, conflict over a 'single' issue threatens his 'way of life,' the whole future of the subculture." [30] Having stressed the problematic nature of conflict regulation in deeply divided societies, Dahl sets out the most common ways in which these conflicts have been handled. One way of dealing with intense conflicts—violence or repression—does not constitute successful conflict regulation according to our criteria. A second possibility—secession—commonly involves civil war. A third—assimilation—lies outside the scope of our concerns. It is not a political arrangement or process, and, more

[32]

important, assimilation only operates over the long run, and by that time a severe conflict could easily have gotten out of hand. A fourth—semi-autonomy—has been omitted from our list for reasons already mentioned with regard to federalism. Only Dahl's fifth and sixth possibilities—proportionality and the mutual veto —are also included among our six practices. Dahl does not refer to stable coalitions, purposive depoliticization, compromise or concessions.[31] This comparison of the two lists indirectly suggests that the present one may be complete since it contains a greater number of common conflict-regulating practices than does Dahl's; moreover, Dahl's list does not include any conflict-regulating practices which are not also found among the six practices.

It would thus seem warranted to offer the following generalization as a descriptive hypothesis: *when intense conflicts are successfully regulated, one or more of the six conflict-regulating practices is always employed.* Again, it should be stressed that these six practices do not constitute a classificatory scheme; the hypothesis is descriptive rather than explanatory, even though we have noted how the various practices may effectively contribute to conflict regulation; nor should the hypothesis be read to mean that when one or more of these practices is employed conflict regulation necessarily or even commonly follows.

Ineffective and Dangerous Conflict-Regulating Practices

The above survey not only indicates how intense conflicts are regulated, it also contains some negative implications which suggest that certain practices commonly regarded as effective "conflict-regulating" mechanisms are not that at all. Two such conflict-regulating practices in particular are ineffective—because they do not in actuality contribute to the regulation of intense conflicts; and dangerous—because they exacerbate the conflict and contribute to violent and repressive outcomes.

Take the model of democratic decisionmaking. A quick examination of each of the six conflict-regulating practices would indicate that they all negate, contradict, or modify the orthodox model of democratic decisionmaking. And for good reason. For the democratic model in its orthodox majoritarian form is unsuitable for the regulation of severe conflicts, at least without the addition of one or more of the six nonmajoritarian decisionmaking formulas. According to this normative-empirical model govern-

[33]

mental decisions are a product of free elections in which a widely enfranchised population votes for competing representatives or political parties. The free elections result in a particular distribution of power in the legislature and the executive, out of which emerges a majority party or coalition of parties, endowed with the authority to make governmental decisions which are binding upon the entire population. Calhoun described this model as "government of the numerical majority." Not only is there a greater or lesser incompatibility between pure majoritarianism and each of the six practices, but, according to Dahl, intense conflicts "rarely seem to be handled—for long—by the normal [democratic] political process employed in other kinds of issues. For this sort of conflict is too explosive to be managed by ordinary parliamentary opposition, bargaining, campaigning, and winning elections." [32]

Calhoun spelled out the basic reason for the ineffectiveness of pure majoritarianism in dealing with severe conflicts. If governments are to regulate severe conflicts they must take into account the interests of the entire society, which means those of each segment. But "government of the numerical majority" is an "absolute government" in the sense that it only responds to one segment of the society—the majority segment. If all segments are to be considered, then it becomes necessary to rely upon the broadly inclusive principle of the "concurrent majority." The adoption of the latter denotes a "constitutional government," which "takes the sense of the community by its parts. . . .and regards the sense of all its parts as the sense of the whole." [33] Otherwise the conflict "would continue until confusion, corruption, disorder, and anarchy would lead to an appeal to force — to be followed by a revolution in the form of government." [34] This is not to agree with Calhoun that the "concurrent majority" principle must be embedded in the governmental structure for conflict regulation to succeed; but one or more of the six departures from pure majoritarianism must be applied if intense conflicts are to be regulated.

There are other reasons for thinking that an exclusive reliance upon majoritarianism is not suitable for the regulation of intense conflicts. Certain characteristics of deeply divided societies contradict some of the majoritarian model's major presuppositions, thereby underscoring its ineffectiveness as a conflict-regulating practice. Orthodox democratic theory, which presupposes alternating or shifting majorities, is certainly not applicable to divided societies. Given the conflict's intensity, individuals belonging to a particular segment or conflict group will be adamantly and emotionally attached to "their" political party or parties. And in this kind of electoral arena party leaders rarely seek to broaden their appeals in order to win the support of intractable individuals belonging to the opposing segment. (See below, Chapter VI, for a critical discussion of crosscutting cleavage patterns which are often said to encourage politicians to make appeals across segmental lines.) Not only would they be unsuccessful in such a venture, they would also succeed in alienating many of their own segmental supporters. Lehmbruch makes a similar point when he relates the deep social divisions and political cleavages of Austria, Switzerland, and Lebanon to their "non-competitive patterns of conflict management," such as proportionality and large-scale compromises. "The numerical relations of rival groups [in these societies] are rather inflexible. This means that. . . maximization of votes—an essential feature of competitive political systems—cannot work. Hence, if neither group has a clear numerical preponderance, negotiated agreement appears to be the only possible [solution] if civil peace is to be preserved." [35]

Pure majoritarianism along with highly stable electoral patterns would relegate the minority to the status of Calhoun's "permanent minority." In the context of a severe conflict there would then be the distinct danger of Tocqueville's "overbearing majority" and what Calhoun labelled "absolute government." Moreover, in deeply divided societies a "permanent minority"— whether it be small or large—is not likely to reconcile itself to permanent impotence. Unlike the minority in the democratic model, which is accorded a reasonable chance of becoming tomorrow's majority, a "permanent minority" is unlikely to accept highly unpalatable governmental decisions or procedural rules which invest the majority with the authority to impose its will upon the minority.

Over and above the unsuitability of pure majoritarianism for conflict regulation, the nature and meaning of the vote itself become problematic in divided societies. Democratic theory is inextricably related to the individual majoritarianism first enunciated by John Locke. Majorities are the product of individual votes, each of which enjoys equal weight. Yet conflict groups in deeply divided societies do not generally conceive of equal and interchangeable individuals as the foundation stone of democratic decisionmaking. To them the basic political unit is the segment or the conflict group. At least one conflict group—usually the smaller one—bases its claims and demands upon the equality of each segment rather than on the number of individuals comprising them. The negation of this assertion by pure majoritarianism is likely to hamper the appearance of effective conflict-regulating practices.

Furthermore, underlying the democratic model is the normative and empirical assumption that electoral competition between men, organizations, and ideas is healthy. Not only can contradictory and conflicting ideas and interests be given free rein, they should be given free rein if governmental decisions are to best approximate what is popularly desired and the regime's legitimacy is to be insured. Democratic theory thus neglects those conflicts whose energetic pursuit would lead not to competition and conflict resolution, but to uncontrolled rioting, the politics of the street, the formation of paramilitary organizations, and eventually the complete breakdown of a democratic regime through widespread violence or repression Without some brake upon electoral competition—purposive depoliticization is the most directly applicable of our six practices in this respect—pure majoritarianism would actually exacerbate severe conflicts.

Two points may thus be made about majoritarianism. First, majoritarianism alone is not a suitable conflict-regulating practice. Although the conflict groups' relative electoral strength serves as an important parameter within which conflict-regulating practices and agreements may emerge, what is called for is the combination of majoritarianism with one or more of the six practices. Second, an exclusive reliance upon majoritarianism would detract from conflict-regulating probabilities and even contribute to the conflict's exacerbation.

There is a second negative implication to be drawn from our survey. It might well be thought that one effective conflict-regulating strategy would involve the creation of common inter-segmental loyalties, values, or bonds — a national identity, perhaps. Such an identity may be said to exist when the majority of politicized individuals accord the nation's central symbols, values, and elite(s) greater loyalty then they do to their class or communal segments. Clearly such an identity would be exceptionally important in regulating intense conflicts, especially since few deeply divided societies enjoy its advantages. It might then be said that the list of six practices is incomplete since none of them involves a direct and purposeful attempt to regulate the conflict by creating a set of common loyalties or values. However, there is good reason for this exclusion. For there are two substantial reasons to think that the purposeful creation of a national identity is less than relevant here. It is highly improbable that a national identity could be formed in a short period of time — and only a short time is needed for an intense conflict to get out of hand. And when the attempt is made, successful or not, to instill a national identity the most likely outcome is not conflict regulation, but the further intensification of the conflict, the imposition of repressive rule, and widespread violence.

We can begin to appreciate the improbability of a national identity being rapidly formed, especially in deeply divided societies, when we realize that the process involves both a breakdown of segmental identities and loyalties (at least, in deeply divided societies) and the internalization of new ones. At best the new identity will be fragile for some time, to be rejected during the first major crisis. If the attempt is made to create a national identity quickly, within a period of five, ten or twenty years, there would appear to be only two foci around which it could develop: a set of emotionally-charged symbols or a charismatic leader. Yet emotional attachments are especially erratic phenomena, and their symbolic centerpiece may begin to fade before they are internalized. This happened with colonial nationalist movements only five years after independence. And Weber has given us a persuasive schooling in the brittle and unstable aspects of charismatic authority. Moreover, Weber's arguments that charisma *may* become routinized contain some pitfalls.[36] Which is to say that some political scientists and political elites in non-western societies have been unrealistically optimistic in believing that segmental loyalties can be erased and replaced with national loyalties in a short period of time. The most that can be hoped for is the addition of national loyalties, building upon or only slightly modifying segmental loyalties.

If, nevertheless, a charismatic figure or emotion-charged symbols are used in an attempt to form a national identity, there is the very real danger that the outcome will be repressive rule rather than conflict regulation. In purposefully attempting to shape common loyalties to the leader or the symbol, the leader or the wielders of the symbol (usually the party) almost invariably claim to be the embodiment of the nation and thus to stand

[37]

above the nation. Such a claim is closely bound up with the Rousseauistic notion of the general will, which dictates that there be no partial and independent groups and associations in the society since these would distort the general will. Unity thus comes to mean the eradication of segmental and other group attachments because only the leader(s) represents the general will.

In attempting to create a national identity it is most common for the leader or the party to claim that it stands "above" the nation. When this claim becomes more than rhetoric, repressive rule is likely to be imposed, as in Ghana during Nkrumah's rule. As part of his attempt to create a national identity in a tribally divided society Nkrumah turned an open regime into a closed regime. In the last five years of his increasingly repressive rule practically all political and nonpolitical associations were banned, or penetrated by his party; the few that survived were saddled with a subversive label. In Nkrumah's oft reiterated declaration, "The Convention People's Party is Ghana, and Ghana is the Convention People's Party." [37] The close relationship between the rapid creation of a national identity and the onset of repressive rule is also found, in somewhat starker form, in Guinée, where Sékou Touré went further than Nkrumah in directly attacking tribal loyalties in both society and the ruling party. The society was penetrated, organized, and led by the Parti Democratique de Guinée, so that "all interests and groups. . .[are] closely interlocked with the structure of the ruling party." Touré himself has made it clear that he regarded individual and group liberties as having validity only insofar as "they promote the realization of the sovereign popular will, again as expressed by the PDG." [38]

Rather than relying only upon a charismatic leader or emotion-charged symbols, it might be plausible to contend that the use of the past—of a country's traditional symbols and values— could be effective in forming a national identity without exacerbating an already intense conflict. Yet the resurrection of tradition, which is often thought of as a calming and unifying factor, becomes just the reverse in deeply divided societies. In such societies there will either be two mutually repellent traditions, or, if only one segment "has a past," the opposing conflict group will be sure to react sharply to the acceptance of its opponents' traditional values or symbols. Ceylon provides a telling example of this point. During the first years of independence the Ceylonese regime maintained its legitimacy on the basis of a western-ized securalism; the country's mutually hostile communal groups (the Tamils and Sinhalese) were able to accept the regime because of its "official disregard for all indigenous cultures"[39] This course was sharply reversed in the middle 1950s. "The search for a common cultural tradition to serve as the content of the country's identity as a nation," according to Geertz, "led only to the revivification of ancient, and better forgotten, Tamil-Sinhalese treacheries, atrocities, insults and wars."[40] The widespread communal rioting and violence of 1956 and 1958 were in large part the result of these efforts.

Not only have none of the elites in our six societies attempted to forge a national identity in anything approaching a sustained and energetic fashion, in at least two of these countries the elites were fully aware of the exacerbating consequences that would follow from such an attempt. In his interviews with the two major Austrian parties' national and regional leaders, Bluhm consistently found the view that conflict regulation could succeed only through pragmatic, low key problem-solving techniques. The party leaders felt "that a great deal of talk about the question of the existence and content of Austrian nationality is divisive and [preferred] more indirect approaches to the building of national feelings."[41] Similarly in Lebanon, where the idea of a Lebanese community or nationality has neither been supported, condemned, nor articulated by the great majority of party leaders. There is little talk about common values or higher principles to which all or most Lebanese should adhere, for such talk would endanger the gains that the conflict groups had realized as well as the regime's stability.[42]

In short, despite the important contribution that a national identity could make to the regulation of intense conflicts, such common loyalties are most unlikely in deeply divided societies; the attempt to create them would in all probability fail; and whether it succeeded or failed, the attempt would heighten the chances of repression and violence rather than of conflict regulation.

Toward a Theory of Conflict Regulation

This survey of conflict-regulating practices also implies an answer to the crucial question: where do we go from here? It points to the critical explanatory phenomenon which is to occupy

[39]

a central place in our theoretical statement. Such a phenomenon is not necessarily the most important independent variable; it need not even be specific enough to constitute an independent variable. Rather, by a critical phenomenon I mean an empirical phenomenon that fulfills one or both of two requirements: many of the important independent variables found outside its confines enjoy their explanatory power insofar as they first affect the critical phenomenon rather than because they relate directly to the dependent variable.

An analysis of the six conflict-regulating practices brings into strong relief the *critical role of conflict group leaders.* In each case of conflict regulation it was the conflict group leaders who took the initiative in working out the various conflict-regulating practices, who put them into operation, and who did so at least partly with the goal in mind of arriving at a conflict-regulating outcome. Furthermore, it is obvious that they, and they alone, were in a position to do so. Clearly the conflict group members (or nonelites) are too numerous, too scattered, too fragmented, too weak, and too unskilled to be able to work out and operate any of the six conflict-regulating practices. In other words, conflict group leaders alone are capable of making a direct and positive contribution to the development and implementation of necessary conflict-regulating practices. The conflict group leaders or elites thus fulfill the first requirement of a critical explanatory phenomenon. It is within the confines of the political elites that many of our explanatory variables are presumably to be found.

If the elites alone are capable of making a direct and positive contribution to conflict-regulating practices, what is the role of the conflict groups — the mutually hostile and politicized nonelites? They are left with three possibilities. They may influence conflict-regulating practices in an indirect and positive manner, an indirect and negative manner, or a direct and negative manner. *An indirect and positive contribution* is made when the nonelites allow their respective leaders to work out particular conflict-regulating practices and then accept them, despite what they may consider their undesirable consequences. The nonelites have an *indirect and negative influence* when they refuse or oppose the leaders' attempts to work out and implement mutually acceptable practices. In neither instance are the conflict groups directly involved. Yet they play a critical part in determining whether or not the elites successfully work out and implement regulatory practices. The elites accordingly fulfill the second requirement of a critical phenomenon as well. While the nonelites clearly occupy a prominent place in any explanatory statement, much of their impact only affects conflict-regulating outcomes after first affecting (or being "filtered" through) the leadership stratum.

Obviously, there is a third possibility, in which nonelites have a *direct and negative effect* upon regulatory practices. The explicit or tacit understanding that nonelites not engage in violence is part of every conflict-regulating practice. Indeed that is one of the leaders' primary objectives. When the nonelites engage in widespread violence, or in hostile acts which escalate to that level, whether at their own instigation or in the face of their leaders' attempts to control them, they can directly nullify proposed or existing regulatory practices. Conflict regulation will then have failed, either directly because of the nonelites' violence, or through the elites' resulting inability to implement the necessary regulatory practices. Of course conflict groups sometimes perpetrate hostile and violent acts with the blessing or encouragement of their respective leaders. But this is to say that the leaders can have a direct and indirect negative impact, which by no means contradicts the assertion that only leaders can make a direct *and* positive contribution to the development and implementation of regulatory practices.

Thus, by beginning with a survey of regulatory practices and then considering its implications, we have identified a critical explanatory phenomenon and laid out most of the major questions that need to be answered and the order in which they may most sensibly be tackled: 1) What elite attributes and characteristics help explain why some elites in divided societies attempt to implement conflict-regulating practices with the goal of bringing about conflict-regulating outcomes? 2) How account for variations in the extent to which elites are successful in obtaining the support or quiescence of nonelites in the implementation of conflict-regulating practices? 3) What are the nonelite variables which explain their acceptance of conflict-regulating practices and the absence of intersegmental violence? Whether or not this theory-building strategy is more than just sensible—whether it is appropriate and useful in searching for some of the most important explanatory variables and in identifying their interrelationships—remains to be seen.

[41]

III

CONFLICT GROUP LEADERS AND
CONFLICT-REGULATING MOTIVATIONS

In the preceding chapter it was said that conflict group leaders are alone capable of making a direct and positive contribution to conflict regulation. It then follows that the leadership must be motivated to undertake such regulation. The presence of strong, salient, conflict-regulating motives among the conflict group leaders therefore constitutes a necessary condition in our theoretical statement. Such motives spring from certain goals desired by the leaders for themselves, or for their conflict organizations, conflict groups, or segments. Only when such motives are present will the leaders engage in conflict-regulating *behavior*, by which is meant any type of activity designed to regulate the conflict, of which the implementation of conflict-regulating practices is perhaps the most important.

Why begin to explain conflict regulation by relying upon the elites' motives, even claiming that these constitute a necessary condition? Because—and most important—unless the leaders are strongly motivated in this direction they may readily succumb to quite different temptations which will actually exacerbate the conflict. Many leaders have a strong motivation not to regulate the conflict, even to exacerbate it, in order to enhance their own positions and those of their conflict organizations. An appeal to the political extremes and to the emotions is an easy, often effective and speedy means to attain greater popularity and support.

[42]

Moreover, conflict regulation is commonly an especially undesirable responsibility. Given the conflict's great centrifugal forces plus the antagonistic and adamant patterns of opposition, conflict regulation becomes a difficult, onerous, and risky enterprise. It also tends to be a rather thankless task. As one sociologist put it, "few men are attracted to tension management and often only the direst emergency will drive them to it. . ." [1] Given all these powerful incentives not to engage in conflict-regulating behavior, we can assume the presence of powerful contrary motives is essential if such attempts are to be made. [2]

In a very real sense the claim that elite motivations constitute a necessary condition is so obvious as to be virtually incontrovertible, yet so general as to be impossible to disprove even in principle. And a proposition which is not potentially susceptible to disproof is not a meaningful hypothesis. It therefore becomes both necessary and advantageous to narrow down and specify the proposition. This can be done by identifying particular motivations which bear upon conflict-regulating behavior and by limiting their number. Fortunately, only four common conflict-regulating motives appear among the elites of our six cases. Nor have I come across additional motives in studies of other deeply divided studies or in the general literature on political integration and related problems. Thus, our first explanatory hypothesis reads: *one or more of the following four conflict-regulating motives is a necessary condition if elites are to engage in conflict-regulating behavior.* The hypothesis does not require that both sets of conflict-group leaders be motivated in regulatory directions, although it is obvious that if they are, the likelihood of implementing conflict-regulating practices is markedly enhanced.

Assuming that this hypothesis is valid, we also want to be able to explain the likely presence or absence of the four motives. Under what conditions are each of the conflict-regulating motives likely to be found in a salient and activated form? This question will be asked for each of the four motives. The answers may be viewed as a set of subsidiary explanatory hypotheses in the study of conflict regulation.

Four Conflict-Regulating Motives

The first conflict-regulating motive springs from one of the most venerable hypotheses in the social sciences: *an external*

[43]

threat or danger will submerge internal conflicts. Such pressures on deeply divided societies have frequently served to provide the motives behind elite conflict-regulating efforts. Before turning to some examples, we should note that this is not invariably so. We cannot accept Simmel's categorical statement that the bitterest enemies will join an association (i.e., regulate their conflicts) "if this association is directed against a *common* enemy."[3] When one conflict group does not value the national regime, preferring secession or incorporation into another state, or when the differences between conflict groups are more salient than the differences between one conflict group and the external state, we would not expect external pressures to give rise to conflict-regulating motives.

This was the situation in the first Austrian Republic. That recently established regime was without a national tradition, nor did it inspire national feelings and loyalties among the Catholics, many of whom adopted a strongly pan-German orientation. In this context Germany's pressures for *Anschluss* only succeeded in exacerbating the Red-Black conflict. In the 1930s many Catholics certainly preferred to live as Germans to living alongside the anticlerical Socialists. In Belgium, given Flanders' cultural and linguistic affinities with Germany and Wallonia's similar attachments to France, each world war helped mitigate the class conflict, but exacerbated the linguistic-regional conflict.[4]

External pressure did, however, promote the Lebanese National Pact of 1943, which initiated the most important and enduring conflict-regulating practices. (It was negotiated between those two leaders of the Christian and Muslim conflict groups who were to become the first President and Prime Minister of the country.) The negotiators' main motives involved the realization of Lebanon's independence—to throw off the French mandate and to become a sovereign state. "All other deeper problems of Lebanese life and society were subordinated to this overwhelming concern. Deep social issues could divide but the pressing need was for unity behind the overall goal of national liberation."[5]

External pressure was also important in the Austria of 1945. The Grand Coalition and the use of the *Proporz* principle were both responses to the presence of Soviet occupation forces. Recognizing that their mutual goals of preventing Russia from carrying off their industrial infrastructure and of avoiding Soviet domination and rapidly terminating both Soviet and Allied occu-

[44]

pation required national unity, the leaders of the two *Lager* were readily motivated to reach a conflict-regulating agreement.[6]

The mutually perceived need for national unity in the face of external pressure also existed during Belgium's first two decades of independence. Lorwin writes that, despite their mutual antagonisms, both Catholic and Liberal leaders "had drawn the great lesson of mutual tolerance from the catastrophic experience of the Brabant Revolution of 1789, when the civil strife of their predecessors had so soon laid the country open to easy Hapsburg reconquest." [7] It was in large part these mutual objectives of securing their small country's borders and its independence that led the two conflict groups to continue their "union of the oppositions" and to work out a compromise on the church-state issue.

Holland's conflict-group leaders had begun working out a compromise to regulate the severe religious and class conflicts prior to the outbreak of World War I. But when the war actually raged around Holland, their efforts were speeded up and perhaps facilitated, leading to the writing and ratification of the national pact in 1917.[8]

Finally, the Swiss confederation originated in the mutual desire of heterogenous communities to preserve their individual independence through a mutual security arrangement. Three centuries later that goal continued to influence the behavior of Swiss elites. A major motivation behind the Protestant offer of concessions to the Catholic cantons after the Sonderbund War was the realization that a country surrounded by more powerful neighbors required a unified and centrally controlled national army. And to insure this unity and central direction conciliation of the Catholic cantons seemed the optimum strategy.[9]

From these examples we can infer that external pressures generally inspire regulatory motives. But these motives are likely to be highly salient, and thus activated, primarily among the elites of states occupying a low rung on the international power ladder. In each of our examples, the state in which conflict-regulating motives arising from external pressure were activated was significantly weaker than the state exerting the pressure: Lebanon vs. France, Austria vs. Russia, Belgium vs. the Netherlands and the great powers, Holland vs. Germany, Switzerland vs. the German states, France, and the Hapsburg Empire. This is hardly surprising. For the weak states provide inviting "targets" for their more powerful neighbors. At the same time, their military weakness sharply underscores the need for national unity in order to fend off the stronger states' pressures. Larger, more powerful states, are more often on the international offensive. And in general, being forced into a defensive position inspires a greater need for unity than the assumption of an offensive posture. Thus conflict-regulating motives arising out of external threats are most likely to be found among the elites of small states.

The belief that *intense conflict and its actual or possible consequences will detract from the economic well-being of the leaders' segment or conflict group* is the second conflict-regulating motive. It is thought that the present level of economic prosperity is threatened, or that economic growth is impossible, because of the conflict's consequences. These may include a climate of economic and political uncertainty, violence, a division of the economy into its geographical parts due to secession, governmental instability, governmental *immobilisme* on economic questions, or the dissipation of productive economic energies into unproductive clashes between conflict groups.

This motivation seems to have been present in Belgium from the time it achieved its independence from Holland. The motivations of the Catholic and Liberal parliamentary leaders, who between 1831 and 1847 worked out conflict-regulating compromises on the religious and educational conflicts, were largely economic. "Unionism was conservative. It was better for business, its advocates thought, than 'sterile discussions' of 'vain ideological questions.'" [10] Later, in the years before World War I, the intense class conflict centering on the suffrage issue was in part regulated because of the anticipated economic costs to the bourgeoisie had the 1913 general strike and other disruptions continued.[11] And in the midst of the current Fleming-Walloon conflict even the Socialists, with their important electoral base in depressed Wallonia, have an economic motive for regulating the conflict, since they believe that the financial resources needed for rejuvenating a stagnant economy and outdated coalfields are more likely to be forthcoming through cooperation between the two conflict groups.[12]

The Swiss Protestant leaders' grant of concessions to the Catholic cantons in 1848 resulted in large part from the belief that a regulation of the conflict would promote the country's economic development. Only a united country governed by a stable regime would be able to remove internal tariffs and trade restrictions and standardize the currency.[13] Although considerably less salient than the goal of ending Russian occupation of its eastern territory, economic motives also played a part in the formation in 1945 of Austria's Grand Coalition. Both sets of conflict group leaders were influenced by the need for postwar reconstruction and the desire to make maximum use of Marshall Plan aid.[14]

Economic motives have also played a prominent role in regulating the Chinese-Malayan conflict. The Chinese political leaders have been concerned with the maintenance of Chinese economic predominance which, given the Malays' political predominance, necessitated mutual adjustment. The Malay leaders, for their part, have been trying to open up economic opportunities in the modern sector for the economically underpriviledged Malays. Short of more drastic measures which would intensify the conflict, such as nationalizing Chinese businesses, the only way for the Malays to gain their economic goal is by cooperation with Chinese businessmen-politicians, that is, by trading a share of political power for economic values. This trading arrangement is carried out on an *ad hoc* year-to-year basis, the Malays granting language and other concessions to the Chinese in return for various preferences and quotas favoring Malay employment in commercial and modern enterprises, the reservation of places in educational institutions designed to train future technicians and managers, and the "distribution" of stock shares to some Malay politicians.

In trying to suggest where highly salient economic conflict-regulating motives are most likely to appear one answer is fairly obvious: in the presence of a commercial class. But this answer remains too broad. The commercial class must also be relatively sizeable and dedicated to the pursuit of greater economic values rather than to their preservation alone — a dedication not found in every commercial class. For example, the nineteenth century German *haute bourgeoisie* was more concerned with attaining social acceptability at the Kaiser's court, which required a denigration and minimization of their commercial activities, than in increasing their wealth. During the Third and Fourth Republics the French middle class evidenced a greater concern for the preservation of their businesses, these being valued for the security and solidarity they provided for the family, than for economic expansion. A commercial class dedicated to expansionist eco-

[47]

nomic pursuits will be able fully to appreciate the intimate relationship between its economic goals and political order and governmental stability; because of its numbers and economic power it will have extensive influence with the conflict group leaders. And insofar as it is safe to assume that a sizeable and dedicated commercial class will be relatively wealthy, another reason may be offered in support of the hypothesis: men are more strongly motivated by the prospect of losing values they enjoy or are sure to enjoy in the very near future, than by hopes for the realization of desired values at some distant time.

A third regulatory motive is the *acquisition or retention of political power.* Up to this point little attention has been paid to the fact that in open regimes most conflict groups give rise to a particular type of conflict organization, namely, the political party. Parties are more or less extensively structured organizations led by politicians who want governmental office, a share in governmental power, and, in many instances, the accompanying financial and status perquisites. In certain types of situations these motivations may lead party leaders to regulate conflict. In addition, electoral considerations may sometimes motivate party leaders to dampen the conflict's intensity.

In Malaysia, for example, the desire for governmental power and office promoted conflict-regulation in a number of ways. The stable governing coalition already mentioned was formed just before the 1952 municipal elections in which the Malayan Chinese Association was fully expected to win majorities in most of the cities. It was partly this expectation of Chinese success which prompted the leaders of the Malay party (UMNO) to form the electoral alliance, later translated into a governing coalition at the time of independence. The Malays were also motivated to ally themselves with the Chinese conflict organization because electoral success required campaign funds, and their only likely source was the wealthy Chinese business community.[15] For its part, around 1955 the Malayan Chinese Association moderated its rigid insistence on the immediate attainment of all Chinese objectives because the leaders realized that no exclusively Chinese party could ever win a legislative majority. In order to enjoy governmental power and offices the Chinese had to remain in the Alliance.

To turn to Belgium, its *fin de siècle* period saw a sharp intensification of the class conflict. Its regulation is partly attrib-

[48]

utable to the Catholic leaders' compromises on social and economic questions; these compromises, in turn, were the product of their desire to maintain themselves in power. It was expected that the expansion of the suffrage, by now imminent, would multiply the Socialists' electoral strength in the Walloon cities, thereby threatening the Catholics' predominance in the legislature and the cabinet It was this spectre of Socialism, not just a religiously inspired social idealism, which prompted the emergence of a Catholic left (i.e., Christian Democracy) in the parliamentary party. The Catholic left faction tried to persuade the party leaders to modify their anti-Socialist program, counseling electoral expediency in order to ward off the Socialist onslaught. For some years the conservative Catholic leaders remained adamant. Only after 1900—in order to maintain their declining governing majority in the Chamber—were the party leaders motivated to meet the Catholic left half-way on social and economic legislation. These two closely related factors—electoral expediency and the retention of governmental office—motivated the Catholic leaders to pass compromise social legislation which helped regulate the class conflict in the years before World War I.[16]

The regulation of the highly-charged school issue in Belgium also resulted from a series of compromises. The most important one took place in 1958, largely as the result of electoral considerations. In the middle 1950s more and more Socialist leaders had become convinced that their anticlerical position on the school conflict was bringing them poor electoral returns, while serving as a catalyst for the Christian Socials. This was born out by the 1958 election, which dealt a sharp blow to the Socialist-Liberal coalition which had governed from 1954 to 1958. As a result, the Socialists agreed to the School Pact, hoping thus to be able to appeal to more Catholics.[17] Similar considerations swayed the Liberal Party. Anticlericalism was not serving it well in its quest for governmental power, winning the support of only 12 per cent of the voters in 1958. Reforming itself into the Party of Liberty and Progress in 1961, the former Liberal Party dropped its ancient anticlericalism and welcomed believers into its ranks, going out of its way to include them among its parliamentary candidates. In 1965 the Party more than doubled its parliamentary strength by taking many right-wing votes from the Christian Socials.[18] In Belgium anticlericalism and the religious dimension of the school issue have since lost their intensity as conflict issues.

[49]

In the Netherlands, the "national compromise"of 1917 which regulated the severe religious and class conflicts occurred in part because of a desire for governmental power and office. In this large-scale "package deal" the Socialists realized the working-class objective of universal suffrage; Protestant fundamentalists and Catholics won state subsidies for religious schools. The Liberals, who had opposed both measures because their middle-class supporters were already enfranchised and deeply committed to the separation of church and state, wanted to call a halt to their continual electoral decline. This could be—and was—achieved through the introduction of proportional representation to replace the single-member plurality system of voting which was helping to decimate the party's electoral and thus parliamentary strength. Thus, in return for proportional representation, the Liberals agreed to the major conflict-regulating compromise in modern Dutch politics.[19]

The desire to retain or acquire governmental offices and power is very common among leaders of virtually all political parties. Yet this motive does not always, or even regularly, lead to regulatory behavior. As our examples suggest, the variation is largely accounted for by the distribution of political power. The desire for governmental power is most likely to engender regulatory behavior when no one party has sufficient support to govern alone. When all parties are minority parties, the leaders are most likely to try to attain governmental power by dampening conflict. In contrast, where there is a sharply unbalanced power distribution the leaders of the predominant party have less of a political incentive to engage in regulatory behavior. They already enjoy the fruits of office. The minority party leaders would then have some incentive to regulate the conflict in order to win more votes or to qualify as coalition partners. But they would not be given the opportunity to act upon their regulatory motives because their support would not be needed by the majority party. A qualification is, however, needed if we are going to suggest that the balanced distribution of power enhances the likelihood of politically inspired regulatory motives. That distribution must appear to be fairly stable. When it seems that no political party will soon achieve a position of predominance, the leaders have more incentive to decrease the distance between conflict groups. In a more fluid context such incentives may be shelved in the expectation that one's own conflict group will enjoy a predominant position at a later date.

[50]

The fourth conflict-regulating motive results from the high value elites place upon the *avoidance of bloodshed and suffering* within their own segments. This motive may be related to a genuine concern for the safety of the segments. It might also be due to a desire on the part of elites to avoid the diffuse risks and unknown dangers of extensive political instability and uncontrolled violence.

For example, we have already noted that at the outset of the Sonderbund War the Swiss Protestant elite selected as their commander-in-chief a man who could be counted on to pursue a military strategy which would minimize bloodshed.[20] Avoidance of bloodshed was also a powerful motive leading Austria's two parties to create the Grand Coalition. Engelmann aptly characterized the elites' motives in this regard when he wrote that the two Austrian Republics "had developed under conditions of cleavage so deep as to leave [them] with a high potential for—and a sporadic actuality of—civil war. The grand coalition must be viewed as an effort to establish minimum consensus in the face of this cleavage."[21]

In Lebanon the conflict-group leaders have been well aware of the country's explosive potential; they know that even a minor incident involving an insult to one of the religious sects could unleash uncontrolled Christian-Muslim violence. In the face of this omnipresent danger, the Lebanese elites have "exhibited an unusually high degree of responsibility" in their conflict-regulating efforts. We have already noted how their regulatory practice of purposive depoliticization is specifically designed to avoid intersegmental strife.[22] In Malaysia the likely possibility of major outbursts of intercommunal violence prompted both Malay and Chinese leaders, but especially the Malay, to form the Alliance and to continue it down to the present. Indeed, the 1969 Alliance Election Manifesto explicitly states that the Alliance exists in order to forestall the realization of those widespread fears of "an irreversible process of disintegration with all the consequential carnage too heinous for anyone to envisage."[23]

These examples suggest that elite motives for avoiding civil strife are likely to be highly salient when the possibility of widespread violence appears most probable. And it would seem that the danger appears closest when widespread civil strife has occurred recently, as in Switzerland and Austria, and when there have been recent sporadic outbreaks of rioting and violence, as in Lebanon and Malaysia.

[51]

A second factor underlying the bloodshed-avoidance motive has been suggested with regard to Malaysia, but, if valid, it is certainly more widely applicable. Esman has applied the concept of mutual deterrence to Malaysia, where "both the Chinese and Malays are strong enough to inflict unacceptable damage on the other, and both sides recognize and appreciate this possibility." [24] While this point appears persuasive, indeed it is frequently made in conflict studies, I would not include it as a condition underlying the strife-avoidance motivation—for the simple reason that a situation of mutual deterrence exists in most intensely divided societies. One underlying reason for the conflict's intensity is the great relative strength of each of the conflict groups, which makes it virtually impossible for either of them to achieve their aims. And in the small proportion of intensely divided societies where one conflict group is clearly predominant, the leaders of the distinctly weaker conflict group sometimes place a high value upon strife avoidance since it is their own segment that could suffer most. Esman's hypothesis may have some validity when applied to the leaders of clearly predominant conflict groups who might be less concerned with strife avoidance because their own segments would presumably suffer less. But, even if valid, it would apply only to a small proportion of deeply divided societies (those in which one conflict group clearly predominates), and in these societies only to the leaders of the predominant conflict group. It would only allow us to make the exceptionally weak statement that strife-avoidance motives occur *less* frequently among leaders of predominant conflict groups than among leaders of distinctly weaker or equally strong conflict groups.

Summary

Our initial hypothesis can now be stated in a testable form which is potentially susceptible to disproof: *the strongly felt presence of at least one of the four motivations is a necessary condition for explaining attempts by conflict-group leaders to regulate intense conflicts.* A corollary is obvious. The probability that leaders will engage in conflict-regulating behavior is increased when they experience more than one regulatory motive. For as was seen in several of our cases, conflict group leaders did exhibit two or three different kinds of motives. Although there are other possible motivations, these are not included in the

[52]

hypothesis for two reasons. To include all possible motives would turn the proposition into an overly broad statement rather than a testable hypothesis. And I am confident that even when other motives play a part in prompting conflict-regulating behavior, one or more of the four motives will be of at least equal salience to the elites.

In developing the motivational hypothesis, four subsidiary hypotheses were also stated which identified the conditions under which each of the conflict-regulating motivations is most likely to appear in a highly salient form among the elites of deeply divided societies. A heavy reliance upon internal unity in the face of external pressures tends to be found in countries which stand at the lower end of the international power ladder. Economic motives tend to be highly salient where there is a sizeable commercial class dedicated to the pursuit of economic values. Motives involving the attainment of governmental office and power are most likely to be activated when no conflict group forms a majority in the present or expects to do so in the foreseeable future. And the avoidance of bloodshed is most likely to be highly valued when the elites believe that civil strife is a very real possibility, these perceptions being found in societies that have already suffered from major civil strife or are experiencing rioting and sporadic violence.

By now I hope to have at least in part reached a number of goals: to underscore the importance of elite motivations in general; to suggest that elites' conflict-regulating motives are a necessary condition in accounting for conflict-regulating behavior and outcomes; to set out the four most common conflict-regulating motives in deeply divided societies; to advance a testable hypothesis which requires the presence of at least one of the four motives; and to offer four subsidiary hypotheses regarding the presence of the four motivations.

In addition, this discussion of motivations implicitly raises the next general question in the theoretical statement's development.

IV

CONFLICT GROUP LEADERS: CONCILIATORY ATTITUDES AND POLITICAL SECURITY

Having underscored the critical role of conflict group leaders, and having stipulated that their conflict-regulating motives are a necessary condition, let us now assume that such motives are present. Yet numerous factors may prevent or encourage the translation of motives into regulatory behavior and of behavior into regulatory practices. It therefore makes sense to try to identify those elite characteristics which can account for such variations. This chapter tries to answer the question: when and why do elites act upon their regulatory motives and succeed in implementing conflict-regulating practices?

Conciliatory Attitudes and Regulatory Behavior

Political scientists have come to appreciate the importance of the political culture in shaping behavior. But they have focused very heavily upon the nonelite's political culture, often at the expense of the elite's. As Daalder put it, "the elite culture is in itself a most important independent variable which may go far to determine how cleavages are handled in a political society, to what extent they become loaded with political tension, and to what degree subcultural divisions are solved in a spirit of tolerance and accommodation or by violence and repression."[1] Having come this far, one highly relevant, plausible, and indeed self-evident cultural attribute of elites comes to mind: the presence or absence (to put it crudely) of a culturally defined predisposition to behave in a conciliatory manner. In his explanations of various patterns of political opposition—which encompasses but does not coincide with our more circumscribed problem—Dahl attributes a good deal of importance to conciliatory attitudes: "Some cultures emphasize the virtues of cooperating with others, conciliating opposing views, compromise, willingness to submerge one's own special ideas in a larger solution." [2] Conciliatory attitudes may be defined as stable and internalized predispositions to view political compromise as respectable, combined with a willingness to bargain with and accommodate opponents.

Our hypothesis is direct and simple: conflict group leaders who subscribe to conciliatory attitudes tend to engage in conflict-regulating behavior much more readily than leaders who do not. It is also much more likely that regulatory efforts will be translated into effective conflict-regulating practices (but not necessarily outcomes) when such attitudes are present. Conciliatory attitudes permit elites to deal with each other less antagonistically, and thus more effectively, assuming of course, that they are motivated toward regulatory outcomes. As in the case of conflict-regulating motives, the hypothesis is applicable to conflicts in which one or both sets of elites adhere to conciliatory attitudes. When both do so the probability of the two-fold translation occurring is significantly enhanced.

On the other hand, even when conciliatory attitudes are present among both sets of elites, regulatory behavior and practices by no means necessarily follow. In the social psychologists' stimulus-organism-response (S-O-R) model, the stimulus does not always lead to a particular response even though the cultural attitudes embedded in the organism have a strong impact in shaping the responses. There are other factors which can sometimes neutralize or contradict the influence of the internalized orientations. This is especially the case in a deeply divided society. The conflict acts as a stimulus which, after being filtered through the positive attitude toward conciliatory behavior, prompts a conciliatory response. Elites are influenced by so many contrary stimuli, motives, demands and attitudes that a regulatory response does not necessarily follow from conciliatory attitudes alone. Yet the hypothesis does enjoy considerable explanatory power in predicting regulatory behavior when the appropriate motives are also present. When conflict-regulating motives are salient, conciliatory attitudes significantly increase the probability that regulatory behavior will occur and regulatory practices be implemented.

This direct, simple and highly plausible hypothesis encounters two difficulties. The first is methodological and affects all hypotheses relying upon political attitudes in explaining political behavior. Attitudes cannot be identified independently of behavior; attitudes can only be inferred from behavior. The not uncommon failure to recognize this difficulty has produced tautological generalizations, in which the behavior to be explained by the underlying attitude is itself used as evidence for the latter's existence. And in turn, this tautologically determined attitudinal variable is used to explain the behavior which originally served to indicate the attitude's presence.[3] In the present study, the hypothesis that conciliatory attitudes contribute to conflict-regulating behavior is circular when conflict-regulating behavior is taken as evidence of the existence of conciliatory attitudes, and these are in turn used to explain regulatory behavior.

Although it is virtually impossible to identify internalized predispositions without some form of behavior—even responding to a questionnaire constitutes behavior—the difficulty may be circumvented by inferring the presence of conciliatory attitudes from elite behavior that does not involve relations between conflict groups. If it can be shown that elites engage in conciliatory behavior in a number of other spheres, then we may fairly safely infer that conciliatory attitudes are present; these may then be used to account for conflict-regulating behavior. While it is possible to establish the presence of conciliatory attitudes in more or less indirect ways, this sort of methodologically self-conscious analysis has rarely been pursued. Therefore, if conciliatory attitudes are to serve as an important independent variable we must rely upon statements regarding the existence of such attitudes even though their presence *may* have been tautologically determined.

A second difficulty with this cultural hypothesis is theoretical rather than methodological. Baldy stated, it is not theoretically "interesting." The hypothesis is trite because the explanatory distance separating the independent variable (conciliatory political attitudes) from the major dependent variable (conciliatory political behavior) is not significant; while the two are not identical, they are not far apart either. But since the hypothesis is both highly plausible and important, we should try to make it more "interesting" by inquiring into those conditions which account for the emergence of conciliatory attitudes. These conditions would then be offered as particularly important subsidiary hypotheses in explaining conflict regulation. This type of inquiry is rarely found in political culture or other literature. No political scientist has even drawn up a speculative list of those factors that might be related to the emergence of conciliatory attitudes. One of the very few of such hypotheses suggests that a balance of power between the parties to a conflict, a balance in which no single group is strong enough to dominate another, fosters conciliatory attitudes.[4] Even here the writers have simply asserted the relationship without setting out the linkages between a particular power distribution and the growth of conciliatory attitudes. Moreover, this type of inquiry gets us into the methodological turbulent and poorly chartered waters of psycho-historical explanation, for many attitudes have their origins in a centuries long past. Yet conciliatory attitudes are so widely applicable in explaining elite behavior as well as regime performance, that we should attempt to account for their emergence despite the relative tenuousness of the enterprise.

The Emergence of Conciliatory Attitudes

Before asking how conciliatory attitudes are formed we must say something about attitude formation generally. The psycho-historical model of attitude formation that I want to employ relies upon a synthesis of three theories of human behavior. Although they start from somewhat different premises they end up by saying much the same things regarding attitude formation. Learning theory as developed by Miller and Dollard, behavioral psychology in the work of Skinner, and exchange theory as developed by Homans, offer a crucial statement that is directly applicable to attitude formation, at least after their individual statements have been synthesized.[5] The statement is: The more frequently a particular stimulus has prompted a certain behavioral response which is rewarded, the greater the probability that this behavior will be repeated in the future when the same stimulus appears. There are two corollaries to this central statement, both of which apply only when the previous statement holds: behavioral responses tend to become repetitive to the extent that future stimuli are markedly similar to past stimuli; and repetitive behavioral responses are positively related to the value placed upon the reward.

This synthesized theoretical statement contains three concepts: stimulus, behavior, and reward. How does it help explain the appearance of conciliatory attitudes among political elites? Conciliatory attitudes are generally activated, and conciliatory behavior usually occurs, in the presence of some sort of conflict situation. For present purposes it is the presence of some sort of conflict involving elites which constitutes the stimulus. Since we are not attempting to account for the growth of conciliatory attitudes in deeply divided societies alone, the conflict stimulus need not be intense. Nor need the conflict take place within an open regime, nor need it involve the nonelite. It could be a nonintense intraelite conflict in a closed regime. The conflict as stimulus then prompts one or another kind of behavioral response, ranging from a resort to violence or the use of force, to implaccable hostility, to conciliatory efforts. Whatever behavioral response is selected, it must be rewarded if the behavior is to be repeated. The rewards would vary according to the behavior selected. For example, the use of force would produce the reward of a military victory or the successful subjugation of the opposition. Clearly this theoretical model cannot predict when conciliatory behavior will occur, nor whether it will be rewarded. Two additional statements are therefore required: something in addition to the conflict itself must act as a stimulus for conciliatory behavior; and this behavior must be rewarded, in the sense that the conflict's outcome underscores the desirability of conciliation.

Over and above the conflict itself, what would serve as a stimulus to prompt a conciliatory response? What would constitute a reward for conciliatory behavior? Actually, we have already discussed the answers to these two questions, at least implicitly. In the previous chapter it was said that under certain conditions regulatory motives are likely to appear. These conditions may now be taken to constitute the specific stimuli (along with the conflicts themselves) which prompt conciliatory behavior, and the realization of the elites' motives becomes the reward which will lead to the repetition of conciliatory behavior. In order to illustrate the utility of this general proposition, and, more importantly, to develop a specific hypothesis, let us select one of the four previously discussed regulatory motives in an extended application of the broad proposition: when the distribution of power between opponents (which need not be conflict groups) is roughly equal and stable, the elites are most likely to act upon their desires for governmental office and power. The presence of this particular power distribution, in which no one group predominates, acts as part of the stimulus to bring about conciliatory behavior, which may be rewarded if governmental office and power are attained.

So far we have not moved beyond our original motivational hypothesis but only restated it in the language of stimulus, response, and reward. If discrete behavior is to be transformed into an attitudinal disposition which consistently prompts a certain type of behavior, then the behavior must be repeated over time and regularly rewarded. This means that the stimulus for conciliatory behavior must be present for at least two generations: the desire for governmental offices and power, for example, remains constant, conflict between the same opponents continues, and the distribution of power between them remains roughly equal for a long time. Under these circumstances conciliatory behavior will tend to be repeated and, if consistently rewarded with governmental office and power, it will lead to conciliatory attitudes as the relevant "lesson" is learned and internalized. In other words, repetitive and regularly rewarded conciliatory behavior engenders the predisposition to engage in conciliatory behavior. A number of factors increase the strength of the resulting conciliatory attitudes. These include the similarity of stimuli over time, the frequency with which the behavior was repeated, the regularity with which it was rewarded, and the value placed upon the reward. Once formed, attitudes, defined as stable, internalized, behavioral predispositions, take on a life of their own. They will thus continue to pattern behavior even after the conditions which originally gave rise to them have been altered. And they will normally be transmitted from generation to generation through manifest and latent socialization processes. We thus arrive at the following hypothesis: *When a conflict in which the* ~~the~~ *no one group predominates is present for two or more generations and the leaders of the groups place a high value upon the attainment of governmental offices and power, conciliatory behavior tends to be repeated and regularly rewarded. This leads to the formation of conciliatory attitudes which continue to influence the behavior of elites during succeeding generations.*

Most if not all students of Swiss and Dutch politics agree

[59]

that conciliatory attitudes have been widely prevalent among the two political elites for at least a century. A recent paper by Daalder traces these attitudes back to the seventeenth and eighteenth centuries. Both countries were characterized by highly dispersed and roughly equal power distributions. Holland existed as the Seven United Provinces and Switzerland took the form of loosely associated cantons. Each emerged as an independent state without a strong central government, without even a central bureaucracy or a central army. (Daalder refers to their "peculiar development of 'sovereignty.'") "Common affairs were decided *ad hoc* by political procedures that resembled international conferences rather than legitimate national governments." [6] As a result, national integration occurred slowly, through a gradual and long-term process of mutual adjustment, without any one economic, communal, or territorial segment providing the primary nation-building impetus. [7]

In the language of our attitude formation model, the elites in both countries experienced similar stimuli: conflict among independent, mutually jealous, regional groupings exhibiting strong particularistic loyalties and interests, a dispersed and roughly equal power distribution, and elite motivations to attain governmental power in order to affect decisions. In both countries these conditions (or stimuli) prompted repeated conciliatory behavior because no single power center was strong enough to dominate the others, and each was usually needed if the confederations were to act at all. The conciliatory responses were regularly rewarded insofar as the leaders of each territorial unit enjoyed an equal share of governmental power, as well as a frequently exercised veto power. Thus, repeated conciliatory behavior along with regular rewards gradually led to the formation of conciliatory attitudes. In Daalder's words, the "traditions of elite accommodation. . .had grown from the necessities of the highly dispersed power structure of the pre-1789 confederations." It is these conciliatory attitudes which may then be used to explain how the elites dealt with their "strong subcultural divisions." They evidenced "a respect for autonomy, a habitual reference to proportional representation, and sometimes a willingness to abide by mutual veto rather than undiluted majority decisions." [8] Secession, violence, and repression have been remarkedly absent in the face of conflicts which might have easily led to such behavior.

[60]

This psycho-historical model of attitude formation may also be applied to the three other conflict-regulating motives. We thus have the hypothesis that conciliatory attitudes are likely to emerge when the elites of a state with a relatively low standing on the international power ladder are experiencing external pressure while an internal conflict is taking place. This stimulus prompts a conciliatory response, which is rewarded by some success in meeting the external pressure. In addition, it is necessary that the stimulus be present for a generation or more so that conciliatory responses may be repeated and regularly rewarded. Conciliatory behavior is then learned and internalized.

To continue with the Swiss case, the long-term presence of a particular stimulus—a state weak in relation to its neighbors, sharp internal conflicts, and the strong desire to preserve its independence—led to repetitive conciliatory responses, which were constantly rewarded in Switzerland's centuries-long ability to remain independent. Many of the linguistically, ethnically, and politically heterogenous communities which made up the Swiss Confederation exhibited considerable mutual hostility. Yet out of the desire to preserve their independence vis-à-vis more powerful states, there emerged during the seventeenth and eighteenth centuries a series of mutual defense alliances which brought the sporadic internal wars to a halt as increasingly frequent conciliatory behavior characterized intercommunity relations. As a result, by the nineteenth century conciliatory attitudes were well embedded in the elite political culture. A Swiss political scientist has said much the same thing:

> In Switzerland, it is common to speak of a true Swiss compromise. . . [which] shows that the norm of amicable agreement possesses a high priority. That such a norm can emerge at all depends partly on its past application having been rewarded. . . .The view is widely accepted that the economic prosperity of the country, its peaceful internal community life, indeed its very existence, are largely derived from the fact that amicable agreement was always aimed at as a means of regulating conflict.[9]

Thus not only did these conciliatory attitudes arise because of international stimuli and rewards; the avoidance of bloodshed and economic prosperity also contributed in a similar manner.

Turning to economic prosperity, the stimulus here is a combination of a conflict which is thought to endanger an economic prosperity much desired by a sizeable commercial class dedicated

[61]

to economic pursuits. Conciliatory responses are rewarded by the attainment of economic prosperity. There is a significant difference between this hypothesis and the two preceding ones because in the latter the motives are directly experienced by the political elites, in whom conciliatory attitudes develop. But economic motives are most strongly experienced by the commercial class, and it is thus among its members that conciliatory attitudes are first formed. This class' conciliatory attitudes must therefore be *transferred* to the political elite if they are to have a political impact. In most societies with a sizeable commercial class this transferrence is readily achieved; there is considerable overlap between the members of the commercial class and the political elite. The leaders of one major political grouping will also be members of the commercial class. In other societies, the transference may occur because some political leaders will be highly responsive to the goals of their bourgeois constitutents, thereby imbibing a strongly felt economic motive. In yet other societies, some elite members will have been socialized into the values of the commercial class, specifically their economic motives, because of their social origins, which are in the bourgeoisie. In short, the emergence of elite conciliatory attitudes due to economic motives requires an additional (but not uncommon) step which is unnecessary when attitudes result from other kinds of stimuli and rewards.

The extensive overlap between political and economic groups in the formation of conciliatory attitudes is illustrated by the Dutch urban regents of the seventeenth and eighteenth centuries. They constituted both a political oligarchy and a commercial class dedicated to economic expansion. According to a leading Dutch historian, their powerful economic motives significantly influenced their conciliatory behavior during the violent religious controversies of the period. The regents' religious commitment to Calvinism did not prevent them from seeing that its strident and monopolistic claims as a "political religion" endangered their own economic pursuits. In the face of inflammatory exhortations by Calvinist pastors the regents consequently supported policies of toleration, and in the face of Calvinist mobs they protected religious heretics.[10] The eighteenth-century regents also recognized that the country's internal ideological conflicts were having unhappy consequences for their international trading activities. This stimulus led them to a purposeful deemphasis of the conflicts, and a willingness to "live with" existing cleavages.[11] By

the nineteenth century these conditions had helped form conciliatory attitudes through the process of repetitive and regularly
rewarded conciliatory behavior.

Economic factors similarly contributed to the growth of conciliatory attitudes in Switzerland. Although its political power
was not as extensive as that of the Dutch regents, the Swiss commercial class dominated the politics of the cantonal cities. Aware
of the close connections between economic prosperity and the
consequences of sharp political conflict, the Swiss bourgeoisie
avoided international ruptures which could lose customers. This
recognition produced a neutral posture in international politics.
It also led to the acceptance of internal divisions and conflicts,
rather than hostile and implaccable reactions along with efforts to
defeat the oppositions.[12] We have already noted that Swiss
efforts at dealing with their conflicts in a conciliatory manner were
regularly rewarded by economic prosperity.[13] Thus, over a period
of two centuries these conditions and considerations helped form
elite political cultures in the Netherlands and Switzerland characterized by the acceptance of particularistic loyalties and segmental divisions, as well as conciliatory attitudes in dealing with
conflicts.[14]

Having attempted to offer some reasonably persuasive explanations for the emergence of conciliatory attitudes, I should
like to point out why they may be considered especially tenuous.
In the absence of any theoretical work on the historical formation
of conciliatory attitudes I relied upon a synthesis of the three
widely accepted theories of human behavior mentioned earlier.
But, since they were not specifically designed to explain the historical emergence of attitudes, their application here may not be
fully warranted. Some very troublesome methodological difficulties afflict all psycho-historical statements; these have not been
mentioned here, much less circumvented or resolved. The Dutch
and Swiss examples support the hypotheses, yet there are too
many crucial gaps in the available literature to turn them into
particularly persuasive examples. Finally, even if the hypotheses
turn out to be valid, there may be numerous other conditions
which give rise to conciliatory attitudes: when taken together
with the ones identified here, the latter may not be among the
most important ones. Given the little work that has been done on
this problem, there is no way to estimate just how many other
conditions can account for the growth of conciliatory attitudes.

On the other hand, after having introduced these caveats, I

would claim that this inquiry constitutes a serious first step in explaining the emergence of conciliatory attitudes. If found useful, its applicability will extend beyond the study of conflict regulation.

The Top Leaders' Political Security and Regulatory Behavior

Even if found together with conciliatory predispositions, elite conflict-regulating motives are by no means sufficient to account for regulatory behavior. In fact, because conflict group leaders occupy leadership positions their tendencies toward regulatory behavior may be markedly constrained. What is it about their leadership positions which can help explain whether they will act upon their motives, with or without the additional impetus of conciliatory predispositions? The top leaders' political security may go a long way in answering this question.

The hypothesis to be developed here is applicable to the few top leaders (no more than half a dozen) of the most inclusive conflict organizations. In open regimes these almost invariably take the form of political parties. The top leaders' political security is a product of their relations with other leaders within their own and closely allied conflict organizations, as, for example, in the case of a Socialist party and its trade union allies or a Catholic party and the church hierarchy. Leaders of their own or allied conflict organizations who affect the top leaders' political security may include cabinet members, members of the party's executive committee, highly placed parliamentarians, high-ranking functionaries responsible for the mass organization, the heads of regionally based communal associations, the officers of tribal unions, trade union leaders, and religious potentates such as bishops in Catholic countries.

Political security is thus defined in terms of the relationships between these first- and second-rank leaders and the conflict organizations' top leaders. The top leaders are politically secure vis-à-vis these other high-ranking leaders when they are not faced with significant challenges to their leadership positions and to the authority they exercise by virtue of their formally paramount positions. Challenges to their incumbencies are readily apparent when the top leaders lose their positions, but this measure is not always appropriate since unsuccessful attempts to remove them may nonetheless qualify as significant challenges.

[64]

In other words, leaders may continue to occupy the seats of authority without exercising much power merely in order to remain seated, which entails a successful challenge to their authority. This is one reason for including a second element in defining the leaders' political security. Top leaders are secure when they are able to exercise the authority due them because of their formal positions; they are politically insecure when their authority is sharply questioned. In short, politically secure leaders not only remain in office, they exercise what might be called preeminent and largely unquestioned authority vis-à-vis other leaders in their own and allied conflict organizations.

If this conception of the top leaders' political security constitutes the independent variable, how does it explain conflict-regulating efforts when the relevant motives, and perhaps conciliatory attitudes as well, are present? There are four connections between the two variables. The first begins with a common belief among political actors (whether true or not is irrelevant) that incumbent leaders are indispensable, or at least far less dispensable, when partisan battles are raging. It is one thing to change horses in midstream, it is quite another to do so when the stream turns into a torrent. The leaders' success in maintaining their positions is partly related to their being perceived as indispensable, which is partly related to the conflict's severity. Politically insecure leaders consequently have some reason not to engage in regulatory behavior, for if their efforts succeed in moderating the conflict they will become more indispensable in the eyes of other high-ranking leaders. And inordinately self-serving leaders may purposefully exacerbate the conflict in order to strengthen their positions. In contrast, politically secure leaders need be relatively unconcerned with their own "fall," allowing them to engage in regulatory behavior with considerably less fear of weakening their positions.

There is a counter argument. Could not insecure leaders also strengthen their positions by engaging in regulatory efforts which lead to the successful implementation of regulatory practices? They would then presumably be given some credit for moderating the conflict and perhaps they could also assume a "statesman-like" posture. Moreover, they might be able to enhance their authority in a number of ways by entering into a stable coalition or acquiring governmental positions based on a proportionality arrangement. Perhaps. But looking at the overall probabilities

[65]

the answer is "no." The risks taken by leaders in attempting to regulate an intense conflict are significantly greater than in allowing it to smolder. For one thing, the leaders' regulatory efforts might fail, which would weaken rather than strengthen their positions. Already insecure leaders would certainly succeed in antagonizing other leaders by making such an attempt. It is commonly far safer to fall back on the hard line position held by many, if not most, conflict group leaders and members.

Second, leaders motivated toward conflict regulation are reluctant to act upon their motivations when they believe that such actions may result in a deep split within their conflict group or conflict organization, or an embarrassing failure to gain the necessary support for their regulatory initiatives. An internal split or the public exposure of their minimal authority would have the effect of weakening the leaders' positions. And these two possibilities are most likely to occur when the leaders' initiatives involve some form of accommodation with the opposing conflict group. Once this has been said it becomes obvious that insecure leaders, already anxious about their tenure and authority, will be far more reluctant than secure leaders to take serious risks which could further endanger their positions. There is reason to think that the initial risk is also smaller for secure leaders. Their greater authority means that they will more easily be able to win others over to an accommodative position, thus reducing the possibility of an embarrassing and power-deflating failure. And were they to fail, secure leaders would probably have sufficient "power reserves" to retain their positions, while insecure leaders would be more likely to find themselves dethroned. Thus secure leaders will be more willing to take those risks attendant upon regulatory efforts, and the risks themselves are smaller.

An illustration of the top party leader's political insecurity as it detracted from conflict-regulating efforts is found in the First Austrian Republic. From the Republic's beginning in 1919 the heads of the Social Democratic Party were committed to the democratic regime and the pursuit of their socialist goals through electoral and organizational means. However, the top leaders were very much afraid of being outflanked and of having their party disrupted by a group of high-ranking Socialist leaders with strong left-wing and communist proclivities. This group presented a sufficiently strong challenge to the top leaders' positions and authority to impel the latter to go beyond the reformism in which they believed. In order to bolster their positions and authority the top leaders publicly adopted a revolutionary language, as in their famous Linz party program of 1926, which referred to the expected violence of the class conflict and their own readiness to use force in carrying out their historic mission if confronted with force or illegal acts on the part of the *bourgeois* Catholics. Although the leaders of the Catholic *Lager* were not motivated toward a conflict-regulating outcome, the Socialist leaders' pronouncements only succeeded in exacerbating already formidable antagonisms, out of which emerged a short civil war and a (domestic) dictatorship. "Socialist unity in the face of potential Communist competition or left-wing dissatisfaction was brought at the expense of whatever chances there were of a minimum of national unity." [15]

The next two points take us into the realm of social psychology. Sharp challenges to the top leaders' positions or authority may result in pronounced anxieties over and above feelings of insecurity. Feelings of insecurity are likely to foster behavior designed to maintain the leaders' positions, as noted in the previous two points. Anxiety feelings are both more intense and diffuse, thereby affecting behavior in additional ways. The hostility produced by anxiety feelings is commonly directed at readily available targets than toward the actual source of insecurity, namely, the challengers within the leader's own conflict group. In deeply divided societies such targets are easily found in the opposing conflict group. Somehow the latter are made to bear the brunt of anxiety-dictated hostilities. Furthermore, a diffuse anxiety commonly prompts hostile perceptions of "out" groups, hostile emotions and a pervasive sense of mistrust, which are also focused upon the opposing conflict group as a readily available target. Political insecurity thus detracts from conflict-regulating behavior as insecure leaders sometimes come to exaggerate the aggressiveness of opposing conflict groups; the opposing conflict groups' demands are likely to be perceived as more than strenuously articulated demands, they may be unrealistically interpreted as direct threats and attacks; conflict-regulating attempts by the opposing leaders may be rejected out of hand because of the insecure leaders' feelings of deep hostility and pervasive distrust; and the conflict may be further exacerbated as the insecure leaders direct their aggressive emotions toward the opposing conflict groups.[16] The upshot is that secure leaders are more likely to react to conflict situations in a manner commensurate with the actual level of the conflict, whereas insecure leaders tend to perceive and react to the conflict situation in exaggerated terms. They may even contribute to its escalation.

The last argument has special relevance for the top leaders' first attempt at conflict regulation. Even when the strongest regulatory motivations are present it is not easy to work out effective conflict-regulating practices that have adequate support on both sides of the conflict line. The problems are multiplied in the first attempt at conflict regulation: the relevant practices must be worked out *de novo*, it is not at all certain that the conflict can be regulated, the opposing leaders have little or no experience in dealing with each other, and they have little or no basis for mutual trust. What is required is the ability to work out, and a willingness to accept, innovative conflict-regulating practices. Yet anxiety generally inspires a tenacious attachment to the immediate graspable *status quo* as a means of relieving psychic insecurity; change is rejected because it represents an uncertainty which can only deepen existing anxieties. I would therefore suggest that politically secure leaders are better able to depart from past behavior, concomitantly initiating, working out, and accepting innovative changes, than are insecure leaders who may very well reject innovations out of hand because of an anxiety-dictated rigidity.[17]

The Explanatory Power of Conciliatory Attitudes and Political Security

Considering the four connections between the top leaders' political security and their conflict-regulating behavior, I would attribute an important explanatory role to the following hypothesis: *as in the case of conciliatory attitudes, the top leaders' political security is not a necessary condition for conflict regulation, but, in conjunction with the appropriate motivations, conflict-regulating behavior, and perhaps effective regulatory practices as well will often follow.* Since the same claim is being made with regard to the importance of conciliatory attitudes, what happens when both explanatory variables are present along with the necessary regulatory motives? My answer to this question takes me out on a long limb: the presence of conflict-regulating motives in combination with both conciliatory attitudes and the top leaders' political security constitute a *sufficient* (but not a necessary) explanation for elite conflict-regulating behavior.

Given the ambitious claim being made for this three-fold hypothesis it is important to provide as extensive a rationale as possible. This can be done by relating the hypothesis to another explanatory statement of conflict regulation. If another student of conflict regulation has identified what he considers necessary conditions for its success, and if it can be shown that the three explanatory variables in our hypothesis help fulfill these necessary conditions, then we would have additional reason for thinking that the three variables are especially important and plausible explanatory factors. Such conditions are set out in Lijphart's work in which he identifies four "prerequisites" for what he calls "consociational democracy." [18]

Lijphart's formulation of the problem and our own focus upon divided societies governed by open regimes both go on to try to identify those factors which help determine whether the regime will remain open while avoiding widespread violence. For Lijphart a polity qualifies as a consociational democracy when important political cleavages coincide with distinct subcultures without the mitigating benefits of crosscutting cleavages and overlapping group memberships, with the political elites managing (usually through some form of stable or temporary coalition government) to maintain the regime's democratic stability despite the extensive divisions.[19] There is one important variation in my formulation. Lijphart focuses upon the presence of segmental division in circumscribing his universe, whereas my universe includes only those societies whose segments are embroiled in an intense conflict. Lijphart thus includes in his analysis countries that are not experiencing intense conflicts, such as contemporary Switzerland and the Netherlands, as well as countries experiencing severe conflicts, such as contemporary Belgium, Austria, Lebanon, and pre-1914 Holland. In accounting for consociational democracy (i.e., coalition politics, and the absence of violence and repression) he does not differentiate between the two types of conflict. While his arguments are applicable to both divided and deeply divided societies, we will only discuss their validity as they apply to the latter.

Lijphart's theoretical formulation is made up of four "prerequisites" and six "facilitating conditions." The "prerequisites" refer to elites and the "facilitating conditions" to nonelites, so we

[69]

will only be dealing with the former at this point. The prerequisites are the necessary "behavioral attributes" of those political elites who manage to overcome societal divisions to maintain democratic stability.[20] These behavioral attributes can be easily interpreted as an analytical breakdown of the elites' conflict-regulating behavior into its component parts. They may be viewed as a useful specification of the dependent variable—elite cooperation that transcends conflict lines—standing at the same level of analysis (not explanation) as those conflict-regulating practices set out in Chapter II. And since these are posited as necessary behavioral attributes, if it turns out that the presence of three elite variables helps explain their appearance the importance and plausibility of our hypotheses would also be enhanced. It should also be pointed out that the claim cannot be reversed. The presence of Lijphart's four behavioral prerequisites cannot predict or explain the presence of conflict-regulating motives, conciliatory attitudes, or the top leaders' political security.

As Lijphart sets them out, the four prerequisites follow sequentially. First, elites must be aware of the "dangers inherent in a fragmented system." They must recognize that the conflict could lead to governmental instability or much worse. This is at once the basic and the least important of the four prerequisites. For there is relatively little variation in the ability of elites to perceive what is quite obvious to most people in a deeply divided society, as in Malaysia, where "it is a rule of public life that any issue, however innocuous on the surface, may erupt in perverse communal forms."[21] However, if Lijphart is correct in stressing this point, what variation does exist could largely be accounted for by the top leaders' political security. The ability to perceive political dangers is partly a function of the concern and time elites devote to an assessment of possible destabilizing and violent consequences. When the top leaders are confronted with challenges to their positions or authority they will devote much of their time, energies, and concern to defending themselves against these intraconflict group attracks, thereby detracting from the attention and concern they are likely to show for potential disruptions and violence. Secure leaders have greater energy, inclination, and time to devote to inter—as opposed to intra—conflict group relations.

Second, elites must be be committed to "system maintenance"—which means a willingness to make conflict-regulating efforts in order to "halt or reverse the disintegrative tendencies."[22] Here Lijphart is affirming what we have already said about regulatory motives: they are a necessary condition if regulatory efforts are to be made. However, he does not specify the specific conflict-regulating motives which prompt elites to make regulatory efforts. Which is to say that our hypothesis, which specifies these motives, can be used to account for the elites' commitment to "system maintenance." When any one or more of the four conflict-regulating motives are present Lijphart's second prerequisite will be satisfied.

Third, there is the elites' "ability to transcend subcultural cleavages. . .The leaders must be able to break through the barriers to mutual understanding caused by subcultural differences, and to establish effective contacts and communications across these cleavages." [23] Clearly, both the willingness and ability to do so are significantly enhanced in the presence of conciliatory political attitudes. The top leaders' political security is also relevant insofar as secure leaders are less likely than insecure ones to interpret and react to a particular conflict situation in exaggerated and overly hostile ways. Insecure leaders tend to perceive the opposing conflict group as more aggressive than it actually is, its demands are treated as direct affronts and challenges to the insecure leaders, and if the opposing leaders take conflict-regulating initiatives they are not likely to be taken at their face value. Insecurity hardly promotes better communications and understanding. Furthermore, breaking "through the barriers to mutual understanding" and the establishment of "effective contracts" are not likely to be pursued by insecure leaders whose anxiety detracts from their ability to depart from the past behavior patterns.

The fourth prerequisite is the "ability to forge appropriate solutions for the demands of the subculture. The leaders must be able to develop both institutional arrangements and rules of the game for the accommodation of their differences." [24] Lijphart takes this to be the most important of the four prerequisites. Again, conciliatory attitudes are patently relevant, and I specifically indicated that secure leaders are better able to depart from past behavior patterns and work out innovative practices, whereas insecure leaders are less capable of doing so, and may even reject innovations out of hand because of an anxiety-dictated rigidity.

[71]

This discussion should have heightened the presumed validity and explanatory power of our three-fold hypothesis and enhanced the claim that the presence of appropriate motives, conciliatory attitudes and political security may very well be sufficient in accounting for the elites' regulatory efforts. For Lijphart has stressed four necessary aspects of the conflict-regulating process at the elite level whose presence is significantly affected by one or more of our three explanatory variables.

INTERNAL CONFLICT GROUP RELATIONS: THE STRUCTURED PREDOMINANCE OF ELITES

We have established the crucial role of conflict group leaders. They alone can initiate, work out, and implement conflict-regulating practices, therefore they alone can make direct and positive contributions to conflict-regulating outcomes. In the last two chapters we identified a number of variables which go a long way toward explaining whether the elites will make such contributions. As for the nonelites, or conflict group members, it was previously noted that they can affect conflict-regulating outcomes in three ways: by indirect negative reactions, by indirect positive reactions, and by direct negative reactions. The indirect reactions involve the conflict group members' support of or opposition to their leaders' regulatory efforts; the direct negative reaction refers to violent action by the nonelite, carried out spontaneously or contrary to their leaders' wishes. In this chapter we shall try to account for the nonelites' direct and indirect reactions by focusing upon elite-nonelite relations.

A necessary condition for conflict regulation is a form of structured relations between leaders and nonelites in which the leaders are clearly predominant and their demands regularly fulfilled. Leaders must enjoy extensive independent authority to take actions and make commitments without being accused of ignoring, dominating, or coercing their followers. This is not to say that structured elite predominance necessarily or even usually involves the subjugation of nonelites. Structured elite predominance is usually tempered with a good measure of responsiveness to nonelite wishes and demands. In open regimes nonelites generally set distinct outer limits to their leaders' demands and control.

The Argument for Elite Predominance

This hypothesis is readily deducible from our theory as developed so far. For if elites alone are capable of making a direct and positive conflict-regulating contribution, it follows that the probability of regulatory outcomes is increased when nonelites consistently accept their leaders' demands. In other words, assuming that elites are interested in conflict regulation to begin with, their structured predominance increases the likelihood of such outcomes. There are other reasons for thinking that elite predominance contributes to conflict regulation, which go beyond this "deduction" from the theory.

First of all, an essential component of the conflict-regulating process is the translation of the elites' regulatory efforts into practices. The negotiation of such practices is greatly facilitated by elite predominance. As Dahrendorf put it: "so long as conflicting forces are diffuse, incoherent aggregates, [conflict] regulation is virtually impossible. . . .One cannot negotiate with unorganized, loosely connected 'rebels'; for conciliation comprehensive organization growing out of a quasi-grouping is indispensable." Furthermore, conflict-regulating practices are not likely to be successfully negotiated when the opposing leaders cannot within reason guarantee that their followers will accept a conflict-regulating agreement. Nor are elites likely to risk severe damage to their power, prestige, and future effectiveness as conflict group leaders by negotiating an agreement which is likely to be rejected by either conflict group.

Then, too, negotiated conflict-regulating practices must be accepted by the nonelites; or at least they must not sabotage the agreements, or violate their intent by engaging in hostile or violent acts against the opposing segment. Translating elite-negotiated practices into conflict-regulating outcomes is not easy, since even a few sufficiently outraged individuals might be able to negate the elites' efforts and intentions. And any conflict-regulating practice is very likely to engender some pronounced dissatis-

[74]

faction at the nonelite level. Thus, benefits may not always outweigh costs. Moreover, nonelite perceptions of benefits and costs are unlikely to accord with the leaders' assessments.[2]

The actual or perceived costs may entail foregoing some cherished symbolic values, loss of some expected or hoped for material benefits, reduction in the conflict group's relative political power, and acceptance of some constraints upon the expression of hostile impulses deriving from deep animosities or desires for revenge. Although the nonelites are very likely to realize some advantages from conflict-regulating agreements and the absence of violence and repression, yet they will tend not to view them as especially salient: where violence and repression have not yet appeared, their continued absence would be seen as especially problematic advantages; benefits are likely to be ignored when they are of a collective variety shared equally by the members of both segments; once realized, benefits will be taken for granted; and other advantages will be of an indirect kind or realized only at some future date, making them seem less "real" than the readily apparent costs to be paid. Or to make this point more generally, nonelites maintain a shorter time perspective and greater expectations than elites. This point has been made frequently, even by a writer like Frantz Fanon who extols the nonelites.[3]

There is another reason to attribute a great deal of importance to elite predominance: it enhances the political security of the top conflict group leaders. We have defined the top leader's political security in terms of relations with other leaders of the same conflict group. Yet the predominance of the leadership stratum over the nonelite affects these relations within the elite stratum. If the top leaders are to be challenged by their somewhat lower-ranking colleagues within the leadership stratum, the latter must possess a significant power resource. While the specific nature of the power resource may vary, in one way or another it will relate to the aspiring leaders' ability to gain the support of a sizeable number of conflict-group members, at the same time foregoing their allegiance to the top leaders. Yet, as we shall see, this requirement is especially difficult to meet under the various conditions of structured elite predominance. The latter bolster the top leaders' political security.

A few examples in which elite efforts would probably have been successful in regulating intense conflicts were it not for their inability to predominate over their followers should highlight the importance of this variable. Between 1946 and 1953 Colombia's Liberals and Conservatives killed each other by the thousands every year in a more than active scramble for economic rewards and appointments to governmental positions. The conflict groups were based upon political loyalties of a personal variety and the desire for economic rewards stemming from governmental control. The violence "degenerated" into banditry and the settling of personal vendettas for another ten years after 1953. The relevant point is that as far back as 1947, and then again in 1948 and 1951, the top leaders of the two political parties had worked out mutually acceptable agreements which would have ended *la violencia*. These agreements sought to insure the impartial investigation of any further acts of violence, to guarantee that no reprisals for past actions would be carried out, to institute free and fair elections, and to provide for a stable coalition government of Liberals and Conservatives. Yet the Liberal and Conservative nonelites refused to accept the three regulatory agreements worked out by the party leaders, in part because they believed that neither set of leaders was capable of controlling its supporters.[4] Only the advent of a military dictator in combination with the exhaustion resulting from ceaseless fighting and terror ended the violence.[5]

A second illustration of the hypothesis comes from Ceylon. In discussing the exacerbating effects of the attempted creation of a national identity, I have already referred to the intense Sinhalese-Tamil conflict. On several occasions between 1957 and 1968 the leaders of the two major Sinhalese political parties attempted to moderate this conflict by introducing legislation to decentralize the national government. The Tamil goal of semi-autonomy was to be largely met by de facto linguistic autonomy, the transfer of Tamil civil servants from Sinhalese Colombo to Tamil Jaffna, and by the creation of regional councils. These proposals aroused passionate opposition in the Sinhalese villages, fostered and led by politically active Buddhist monks. They charged that decentralization would "divide the nation" and "deprive the Sinhalese of their legitimate place in the country." In 1957, the Sinhalese Prime Minister, Bandaranaike, came under such heavy pressure from the Sinhalese opponents of the language agreement that he not only gave in to them, he symbolically handed a written repudiation of the pact to Buddhist monks and others demonstrating in front of his residence. This repudiation

[76]

touched off a wave of looting, arson, rioting and atrocities and led to a death toll in the hundreds.

In 1968 the Sinhalese leaders again tried to regulate the conflict by decentralizing the national government and some of its responsibilities. Yet opposition within the Sinhalese conflict group was so widespread that Sinhalese members of parliament also opposed the party leaders in a series of back-bench revolts. Prime Minister Senanayake withdrew the legislation. Thus, despite the Sinhalese party leaders' belief in the moderating influence of the proposals, despite their having received the agreement of the Tamil party *leaders*, despite the fact that the legislation had already been written and was about to be introduced, and despite repeated efforts to have the legislation enacted, in each case nonelite pressures forced the Sinhalese leaders to drop the proposals.[6]

The point is reinforced in Nolte's highly-regarded study of the transformation of the Italian democracy into a Fascist state. According to Nolte, this transformation was significantly related to the fascist nonelite's refusal to accept the predominance of the movement's foremost leader.[7] In the years 1920–1921 Mussolini actively worked for the peaceful and nonrepressive regulation of the country's severe class conflict, yet by 1922 he had failed, largely because he was unable to assert his predominance. In an effort to make peace with the left, Mussolini surrendered one of the strongest trump cards held by the Fascists. He publicly recognized that the workers had been defeated; the threat of revolution had passed by 1920. It was this recognition in combination with his regulatory goals that led Mussolini to forbid the *fasci* from undertaking any further punitive attacks against the workers, trade union members and buildings, agricultural cooperatives, and socialist city governments. The order was ignored. Looting, arson, terror and violence even increased as the "squadrists" went about systematically and methodically destroying the opposition in the face of Mussolini's order to use force only in retaliation.

Mussolini's broadest regulatory goals—those of republicanism and social democracy—were also derailed. According to Nolte, Italy's future "was not imagined by Mussolini as 'fascist' at all; in a speech in the Chamber he cited the three great forces which in sincere collaboration must lead the country to a happier destiny: a self-improving socialism, the Popolari, and finally fascism (evidently also to be improved)." His broadest goal

[77]

was still "the constitution of a three-armed Social Democracy." [8] The "squadrists" protested against the speech, won supporters, and mutinied by calling a conference without even a *pro forma* invitation to Mussolini. Perceiving his impotence against the nonelite's transformation of fascism from a liberating into a tyrannical movement, and from that of the nation's guardian to the defender of private interests, Mussolini resigned. It was only after some high-ranking leaders realized that fascism was incapable of getting along without him, that a compromise was worked out and Mussolini was acclaimed the Duce of Fascism. The party captured Mussolini, rather than the other way around. The Fascists wanted to seize power for themselves alone, and they wanted to do so by relying upon force. After 1921 Mussolini successfully directed them in these efforts, although the goals were originally theirs, and Mussolini had strongly opposed them at first.

The Conditions of Structured Elite Predominance

In light of these considerations and illustrations it would seem that the leaders' structured predominance is sufficiently important in the regulation of severe conflicts to warrant its inclusion as a necessary condition. Let us now attempt a limited "test" of our hypothesis by examining elite-mass relations in the six societies we have previously used as examples of successful conflict regulation. Since the hypothesis is stated in the form of a necessary condition we must find structured elite predominance in each case. While the "test" is a limited one, it has not been purposefully biased since our cases were selected before the hypothesis was formulated. If the "test" turns out to be both positive and persuasive it will have enhanced the proposition's plausibility.

I have another objective in mind in taking a brief look at leader-follower relations in the six countries. Over and above illustrating and "testing" the hypothesis we will want to take a further step in explaining conflict regulation. This may be done by setting out the various general conditions which give rise to structured elite predominance. As in our analysis of conflict-regulating motives, it may be that these conditions are few in number, which would allow for an additional explanatory hypothesis: the presence of one or more specific conditions is necessary if elites are to enjoy a structured predominance. Instead of

[78]

discussing elite-nonelite relations in each of the six societies in turn, we shall therefore organize the discussion around the various conditions for elite predominance as they appear in our cases.

Elites may most easily predominate over their followers when they barely see themselves as followers to begin with. In such instances the nonelite is *apolitically quiescent*; it expects to be on. In those instances when the nonelite does become politically involved, it does so at the behest and under the strict guidance of its leaders. This inertness may stem from a diffuse political apathy, but this is not what I have in mind. For apathy sometimes explodes into mass action which cannot be controlled from above, and it is not likely to be widespread in intensely divided societies. Rather, I am referring to that apolitical quiescence which was widespread before the intellectual, emotional, and ideological currents of political activism, engagement, equalitarianism and mass democracy appeared in nineteenth-century Europe. In the absence of such ideas, or in the event of their not having become popularly rooted, elites could initiate, work out, and apply conflict-regulating practices without having to give more than a fleeting thought to the problem of bringing along their followers. Politics was then the exclusive concern of a tiny stratum consisting of high-status, wealthy men and the political elites themselves.

It was in just this climate of apolitical quiescence that the Swiss Protestant elites were able not only to regulate but to resolve the intense religious-territorial conflict by offering the Catholics significant concessions. Although democratic and egalitarian ideas were deeply ingrained in some of the Swiss cantons, in the middle of the nineteenth century they had not yet been transferred to the national (or federal) political arena. Moreover, these ideas were concentrated in the Catholic cantons, whose leaders did not make a singular contribution to the conflict's regulation.[9] Similarly, the Belgian elites' regulation of the religious conflict through the compromises built into the "union of the oppositions" in the 1830s and 1840s could go unchallenged and virtually unquestioned by a nonelite which was not enfranchised and apolitically quiescent in domestic affairs.

Leaders may also predominate over their followers when the latter subscribe to a set of *politically acquiescent or deferential* attitudes. Such attitudes entail the normative belief that leaders are expected to lead and followers to follow. The nonelite gives

[79]

the leaders wide independent authority to act in a manner which they think best, and accepts their decisions even when the non-elite finds them questionable or distasteful.

Such attitudes have been described by students of British, German, Swedish, Northern Nigerian and Japanese politics. They are also found in Malaysia. In that country governments are expected to govern, there is little confidence in the efficacy of participatory institutions, there is no normative belief in widespread participation, and there is much respect and deference, especially among Malays, for persons who represent authority. It is largely because of such attitudes that the two segments have accepted the extensive authority of their "natural leaders," the Malay aristocrats and the Chinese capitalists. The stable coalition between the major Malay and Chinese parties (the Alliance) has largely been founded upon these acquiescent attitudes, which enabled the Malay and Chinese party elites to agree to deliver the support of their respective communities to the Alliance. The nonelite accepted the decisions negotiated by their "natural leaders." [10] Writing in 1971, Esman could say that "the prevailing style of Malaysian politics is still paternalistic, and the party leaders are continually lecturing their members to let the leaders decide issues, including disputes which are not communal." The elites continue to "control the political parties through a process of highly centralized decision-making which has been occasionally challenged but never seriously threatened." [11] These nonelite attitudes not only help shape internal conflict group relations; they also have an impact upon governmental structure and governing style, And as such, they have had an indirect impact upon the conflict's regulation.

> The Alliance insists on its right to determine what issues will be discussed [publicly and within the legislature]. The leadership has constructed a system of governance admirably suited to central control and implementation. Conflict is kept at a minimum; the style is extraction, explanation, exhortation. Persuasion and participation are assumed to have been accomplished with the election of the legislature." [12]

In his study of Dutch politics, Lijphart also stresses the nonelites' acquiescence in their leaders' "oligarchical power," an attitude which stems partly from the stress placed upon deference and obedience in both Calvinist and Roman Catholic doctrine.[13] The diffusion of acquiescent attitudes in Holland was most clearly and, for our purposes, most relevantly manifested in 1917, when the religious and class conflicts were successfully regulated. The proposals which the elites had agreed upon required a constitutional amendment which had to be approved by two successive parliaments. In order not to endanger their successfully negotiated compromise the party leaders "turned the required election between the first and second readings of the constitutional amendments—designed to let the people have a voice in changing the constitution—into a formality. They entered into an agreement allowing all incumbents to win re-election." [14] Rather than reacting against what might easily have been interpreted as an electoral subterfuge, the voters obliged their leaders by returning a parliament which was the exact replica of the preceding one. This parliament then gave constitutional and legislative force to the agreements which the party leaders had previously negotiated.

Leaders may also regularly predominate over their followers when they stand in a patron-client relationship to each other. Clients offer patrons social deference, economic obedience and political support in exchange for highly valued concrete benefits. These may include jobs at the patron's disposal, government jobs secured through the patron's influence, suitable marriage partners, small amounts of money, loans, food, farming rights, and political influence in general. If the conflict group leaders are to predominate over their followers these local patron-client relationships must then be pyramided to the national level. This pyramiding is accomplished by brokers who

> stand guard over the critical junctures and synapses of relationships which connect the local system to the larger whole. Their basic function is to relate community-oriented individuals who want to stabilize or improve their life chances, but who lack economic security and political connections, with nation-oriented individuals who operate primarily in terms of. . .national institutions, but whose success in these operations depends on the size and strength of their personal following.[15]

It has been said that the most characteristic and important aspect of Lebanese politics "is the labyrinthe (sic), shifting factionalism, of local notables with their clienteles of supporters." Each religious sect is structured according to patron-client relationships in which the patrons (or *zu'ama'*) are able to speak and take action in the name of their supporters.[16] With regard to conflict regulation specifically, the *za'im* serves "as a guarantor

[81]

of the peace; he is able to treat with the heads of different groups and to establish some kind of equilibrium between his community and the outsiders." [17] And despite the gradual replacement of landowning patrons by commercially based *zu'ama'*, "sectarian crises are still settled largely through the intervention of the traditional notables, each of whom can calm excited feelings by personal access to his clientele." [18]

Leaders may also come to predominate over nonelites through what is probably the most characteristic feature of modern politics: the mass political party. Yet not all parties provide for structured elite predominance. Only *mass parties with extensive organizational capabilities do so.* Parties vary according to the proportion of party members found among the class or communal segment; their organizational depth, by which is meant the linkages between local, regional, and national bodies; and the existence of well-subscribed ancillary organizations through which the members derive social, cultural, and economic benefits. Political parties with relatively high rankings on these three dimensions allow the leaders to engage in extensive communications with conflict group members; provide a set of political identities and loyalties that places some constraints on possible nonelite tendencies to stray away from the leaders; place the elites in regular contact with the nonelites through the local and regional leaders; and provide nonpolitical benefits, along with the social constraints imposed by membership in ancillary organizations, which gives the members much reason to pause before rejecting the leaders' directives.

It has been said that "the central fact of Austrian political life is the strength and power of party organizations." [19] More than one-third of Socialist voters are paid-up party members, compared with less than 10 per cent in West Germany. The effective membership of the People's Party represents from 25 to 30 per cent of its regular electorate — an exceptionally high proportion for a European Christian Democratic party. Voter turnout exceeds 90 per cent in every one of the nine provinces for national and provincial elections. [20] These statistics are probably unmatched in any other country. In addition, the Socialists and The People's Party possess great organizational depth, with one out of every ten members occupying some official local or regional position, thereby providing the parties with "elaborate cadres of officers and non-commissioned officers." [21] And both parties have more than a sufficient number of ancillary organizations—including, for example, the Federation of Worker Music Societies and the Austrian Union for Gymnastics and Sports—so that a "worker can, and most frequently does, find all of his social needs and intellectual interests satisfied by organizations close to the SPO; the same thing is true of a Catholic layman who is likely to do his social dancing, his lecture-going and his skiing in Church – or OVP—sponsored organizations."[22] In one Austrian town with thirty-seven distinct clubs or associations, mostly of a social, cultural, recreational or vocational variety, thirty-five were related to either the Catholic or Socialist bloc. In a small industrial city, half of its fifty associations had partisan connections.[23]

Belgium's class conflict reached its highest intensity between 1890 and 1920. Its successful regulation was significantly related to the three major parties' extensive organizational capabilities, especially that of the Socialist Party. During this period unions affiliated with the Socialist Party had the kind of organizational capacity which allowed Daniel Halevy to remark that Socialist enthusiasm was French, but Socialist organization was German and Belgian.[24] The extensive nonelite mobilization into the parties' ancillary organizations—at this time public welfare services were first subcontracted to partisan association—led some observers to comment on the multidimensional strengths of Belgian parties. Their organizational capabilities were so highly regarded that they were viewed as estate-like corporate groups. And it was just during this period of organizational growth (and intense class conflict) that the "party leaders emerged as the masters of Belgian politics. . .able to engage in coalition-making and bargaining much as the executives of independent states engaged in diplomacy."[25]

One set of events may be noted which underscores the importance of the Socialist leaders' predominance in regulating the class conflict. The 1902 general strike was a failure because some workers began dynamiting and shooting even before the strike, allowing the Catholic government to call in the police and army and then to ignore the ruthlessness with which they put down the workers. There was another general strike in 1913, with the Catholics again hoping that an outbreak of violence would allow them to use force, and thereby both defeat the workers and drive a wedge between the Socialists and middle-class Liberals who were temporarily allied in the suffrage conflict. However, the

[83]

Socialist Party's elaborate organizational preparations were effective:

> the workers, indoctrinated with the need for absolute discipline, almost entirely refrained from violations of law and order. A special "strike police" had been organized by the party to keep hotheads in line, but found hardly an opportunity to act. The peacefulness of the strike, even more than its extent, made the demonstration formidable . . .Even the most conservative [legislators] seem to have decided that the cost [of not extending the suffrage] would be too high in view of the determination and discipline of the workers.[26]

Although Belgium's class conflict was successfully regulated by the early 1920s, the severe religious conflict centering on the state's role in primary and secondary education continued until the signing of the 1958 school pact. And during this period the Socialist and Catholic parties' extensive organization capabilities were further expanded. By the 1950s the ratio of membership to potential membership in Belgian unions was almost twice that of American unions, and this despite the almost completely voluntary membership in Belgium compared to the not uncommon legal compulsion to join American unions. In Lorwin's estimate, there are only three countries—Belgium, the Netherlands, and Switzerland—in which the unions' organizational capabilities are sufficient to give them a powerful political and economic voice despite the division of organized labor into several rival religious and linguistic movements.[27] The Socialists' organizational capacity extended beyond the party's close links with the labor unions. In order to keep its supporters within the fold the party expanded its ancillary economic, social, and cultural associations, and added other types of associations and services as the desire for them arose over the years. By the 1950s the party had set up retail stores, restaurants, an insurance company, clinics, holiday camps, and rest homes to meet the workers' desires and needs. The Christian Society Party was not to be outdone by the Socialists. By the 1950s it featured ancillary associations of farmers, manual workers, white collar workers, peasants, farm laborers, small businessmen, women and youth, with the Catholic church standing behind all these organizations. Given the lower classes' potential exposure to socialist influences in combination with the relative poverty of their social relations, the Christian Social Party made special efforts to isolate the lower classes within a panoply of ancillary associations. In the 1950s the chaplain of the Belgian Catholic Workers' Movement stated: "A triple idea governs the structure of our great Christian labor organization: that of totality, of complexity, and of unity. . . .Our movement must embrace the whole person of the worker, the whole of the worker's life, the whole family of the worker, all workers' needs, and the whole working class. We want the working man and woman, youth and adult, in coming into our movement, to find everything there." [28]

Thus between 1890 and 1958 the Socialist and Catholic leaders were able to exert a large measure of control over their followers, thereby contributing to the regulation of the class and religious conflicts. But as the linguistic-territorial conflict reached intense proportions in the 1960s these party leaders were not able to elicit the same kind of cohesion from their supporters. For the major parties accumulated their present supporters on the basis of class and religious divisions which do not coincide with the Fleming-Walloon division. Consequently, two splinter parties emerged in the 1960s which challenge the major parties' less-than-extremist positions on the linguistic-territorial issue. Some Flemish Catholics have left the Christian Social Party to join the Volksunie, while some federalist-minded Socialists supported the Walloon People's Movement. However, these splinter parties have not gained more than 16 per cent of the votes cast in any recent election. And with the 1970 conflict-regulating agreement requiring a concurrent majority for the passage of linguistic-territorial legislation there is little reason to think that their numbers will increase—certainly not in the minority region of Wallonia.

It thus turns out that one or another form of structured elite predominance was present in each of our six cases. In fact, it would be more accurate to say eight cases since Belgium featured three severe conflicts during three different historical periods. These last few pages may therefore be viewed as a partial "test" of the proposition that structured elite predominance constitutes a necessary conflict-regulating condition; the hypothesis has at least survived an attempt to falsify it, thereby enhancing its presumed validity. And given the hypothesis' importance—it is stated as a necessary condition—it would seem warranted to use it in further developing the theory.

Rather than suggesting that the four conditions—apolitical quiescence, acquiescent attitudes to authority, patron-client relationships pyramided to the national level, and mass parties with extensive organizational capabilities—are simply illustrative of the various bases of elite predominance, or even claiming that

[85]

these four are the most common bases, the theoretical statement may plausibly be extended by offering a far more ambitious secondary hypothesis: *the four conditions constitute an inclusive list of all empirically realizable bases of elite predominance in open regimes confronting intense conflicts.* We are suggesting that structured elite predominance is a necessary conflict-regulating condition, and if this condition is to be satisfied, one or more of the four bases of elite predominance *must* be present.

Admittedly this is a highly tenuous proposition, based as it is upon six cases, no matter how representative they may be of the universe of successfully regulated intense conflicts. Yet there are some fairly persuasive reasons for thinking that it defensible, and that it should therefore be included in our theoretical statement as a plausible hypothesis. (1) With regard to the wide-ranging applicability of the four conditions, one is especially likely to be found in underdeveloped peasant societies (patron-client relationships) and another is particularly applicable to economically advanced societies (well organized mass parties). (2) Similarly, one of these conditions has special applicability to societies which have not yet entered the era of mass politics (apolitical quiescence and one is probably the most characteristic or distinguishing feature of societies that have already entered that period (mass parties). Thus despite the small number of conditions specified in the hypothesis, they are sufficiently disparate to "cover" great variations in geographical space according to the criterion of economic development as well as variations in historical time according to the criterion of mass politics. (3) The four conditions also cover a wide analytical spectrum of variables. They include two attitudinal variables (apolitical quiescence and acquiescence to authority), a personal face-to-face variable (patron-client relationships), and a formal organizational variable (mass parties). (4) There are other conditions which could be used to account for structured predominance, but they can be subsumed under one or another of the four conditions. For example, structured predominance is sometimes based on the nonelites' dependence upon their leaders for material goods. Yet this condition can be subsumed under patron-client relationships in the case of peasants and under mass parties in the case of economically insecure workers. (5) Other variables could help account for structured elite predominance, but they do so only indirectly, by first helping to attain or maintain one of the

[86]

four conditions. They are more appropriate for explaining why the four conditions are present to begin with. For example, it could be shown that a low level of social mobilization contributes to elite predominance, but it does not follow that low social mobilization constitutes an addition to the four conditions. For a low social mobilization level facilitates elite predominance insofar as it first helps maintain political quiescence. Similarly, it might be suggested that political elites with high social status tend to enjoy positions of predominance. However, it would be more accurate to say that high social status is one among other possible factors which help engender and maintain acquiescent attitudes toward elites. (6) Then there are those factors capable of generating nonelite acceptance of their leaders' predominant positions, except that these factors are not usually present long enough to make for structured, or regularized, elite predominance. Elite success in realizing the conflict groups' goals is one such factor. For it is not unusual for today's victories to turn into tomorrow's ingratitude when additional successes are not forthcoming. Similarly, leadership abilities (whatever is meant by this nebulous term) which are appropriate in one set of circumstances may be quite irrelevant and even disadvantageous when circumstances change. To which may be added Weber's emphasis upon the brittle qualities and temporary nature of charismatic authority — an assertion which has been recently born out in Ghana and Indonesia. (7) Lastly, some conditions which often give rise to elite predominance just as frequently lead to quite the reverse outcome. It has often been claimed, for example, that ideologies promote political cohesion, usually around the most prominent bearers of the ideology (i.e., the party leaders). Yet ideological parties are highly prone to divisive tendencies. Just because so much importance is attached to each article of ideological faith, when discrepancies arise in interpreting their meaning the frequent upshot is party factionalism or fragmentation, as in France, Italy, Weimar Germany and Republican Spain.

To repeat, despite the little evidence from which the hypothesis was originally derived, these seven points are sufficiently persuasive to warrant its inclusion as a plausible proposition. Thus, *structured elite predominance is a necessary conflict-regulating condition, and the presence of one or more of our four conditions is necessary for structured elite predominance in deeply divided societies.*[29]

[87]

VI

THE IMPACT OF NONELITES: SOME POSSIBLE EXPLANATIONS

This chapter deals with those nonelite characteristics which may have a bearing upon conflict-regulating outcomes. As such, it represents a continuation of our "downward" movement from regulatory practices to elites, to elite-nonelite relations, and now to the nonelites themselves. This chapter is informed by the same two questions asked in the preceding chapter. What are the nonelite attributes which have an indirect bearing on regulatory outcomes by making elite regulatory efforts more or less likely and their translation into successful practices more or less problematic? And what are the nonelite characteristics which make it more or less likely that the nonelites will have a direct and negative impact by engaging in widespread violence?

Before getting into the substantive discussion it needs to be said that this chapter differs from the earlier ones in two important respects. First, it deals mainly with hypotheses suggested by others, rather than my own. The literature is rich in hypotheses dealing with nonelite characteristics, but it has little to say about other kinds of variables. Second, this chapter departs from the others insofar as I argue that certain hypotheses do *not* help explain conflict-regulating outcomes. Originally, this chapter was not intended as a critique of the literature. But it seems to me that those nonelite attributes which are often accepted as explanations of conflict regulation are actually incapable of doing so. Therefore a critique became eminently warranted.

If my criticisms are accepted, then two positive conclusions emerge, at least indirectly: if nonelite variables cannot account for conflict regulation, then elite variables become all the more important as explanatory variables; and, to the extent that alternative and competing plausible hypotheses are rejected, the hypotheses already developed in this study come to enjoy a greater measure of plausibility.

The literature contains three types of hypotheses which relate nonelite characteristics to conflict-regulating outcomes. Within the realm of political culture, it is said that the nonelite's positive attitudes toward elite cooperation and the nation facilitate regulatory outcomes. Perhaps the explanatory hypothesis most widely accepted among American political scientists asserts that a conflict's intensity is markedly dampened when politically relevant values form a crosscutting pattern at the nonelite level. And it has been claimed that the likelihood of intersegmental violence is reduced insofar as hostile individuals are isolated from each other.

Political Culture

Political scientists now recognize the importance of political attitudes not only in patterning behavior but in shaping the contours and performance characteristics of regimes as well. Political attitudes refer to particular objects and relationships which have some political content. If we ask what kinds of political objects and relationships relate to conflict regulation, two answers seem to be readily apparent: nonelite attitudes toward the elites' regulatory behavior and practices; and nonelite attitudes toward the nation as encompassing both segments in deeply divided societies. In Lijphart's work, we find two such attitudinal variables. They emerge in his attempt to identify those "facilitating conditions" which help explain "over-arching inter-elite cooperation" (i.e., consociational or conflict-regulating practices) and democratic stability (i.e., the absence of violence and the maintenance of the regime's democratic framework).

In explaining elite regulatory efforts and the resulting practices, Lijphart relies upon "popular attitudes favorable to government by grand coalition," or what he also calls "widespread

[89]

approval of government by elite cartel."[1] As he uses these attitudinal concepts, somewhat loosely, the political objects and relationships to which they refer—"government by grand coalition" or by "elite cartel"—include many of the conflict-regulating practices set out in chapter II above. Thus we have a seemingly plausible straightforward relationship between nonelite attitudes and the elites' implementation of regulatory practices. Yet the hypothesis does not say very much: if nonelites are favorably disposed to certain regulatory practices then elites are more likely to implement them. Despite their touch of circularity such hypotheses could be especially important if their validity and explanatory power were sufficiently important to outweigh their weaknesses. But I do not think that the validity or explanatory power attaching to this hypothesis are especially significant.

In support of his hypothesis Lijphart points out that the two-party system of the Anglo-American variety is "not only a particular empirical type of democracy, but also a *normative* model which may form an obstacle to alternative attempts (i.e., consociational practices) to establish a stable democracy."[2] Popular normative preferences for party competition and alternation in office detract from regulatory practices of the consociational type. In support of this position Lijphart turns to Austria, where, he claims, the Austrian Grand Coalition was under constant criticism for "the 'undemocratic' nature of grand coalition politics, according to the norm of especially British democracy."[3] It strikes me as implausible to attribute such norms to a people who have never lived with "British type democracy." And it is of some significance that the sole reference to this "constant" popular criticism I have seen is only to the months prior to the 1966 election. More important, this criticism was directed against the government's inactivity rather than any violation of normative beliefs in two-party competition and alternation in office.[4] Even if Lijphart were correct in thinking there were such constant normative criticisms on the nonelites' part, I do not see how they could have had an adverse effect on the outstanding conflict-regulating success and twenty-year stability of the Grand Coalition. Nor can it be claimed that this presumed nonelite criticism had a significant bearing upon the coalition's demise. For it was the restive, reform-minded leaders of the People's Party who, disenchanted with governmental *immobilisme,* ended the coalition; and this step was taken only after they were satisfied that the conflict's intensity had subsided so much that national "solidarity" was no longer required.[5] Lijphart's use of Lebanon as a supporting example is also weak. As we have already noted, Lebanese electoral arrangements require legislative candidates to win support from religious sects other than their own. The result, according to Lijphart, is a "largely irrelevant" Chamber of Deputies, the major decisions being made by the cabinet and at extra-governmental elite get-togethers. The assertion of this cause-effect relationship between electoral arrangements and elitist decision-making is both logically and empirically suspect. But even if it did exist, there is a serious problem. Lijphart's assumption that this particular electoral system could not exist without, or that it has helped form, *popular attitudes* favorable to elitist government of a consociational variety does not seem justified.

Despite the weaknesses of Lijphart's argument, there is probably some relationship between positive nonelite attitudes toward "government by elite cartel" and conflict-regulating behavior and practices. At least it is difficult to see why this common sense proposition does not hold even though Lijphart has not offered any valid examples in its support. Yet there are two reasons for not including the hypothesis in our theoretical statement. To the extent that these nonelite attitudes do provide a measure of support for, or at least do not negate, interelite cooperation, this aspect of the conflict-regulating process is already covered by one of our previous hypotheses. There is some overlap between Lijphart's hypothesis and our argument for the importance of structured elite predominance; the latter is not only functionally equivalent to the former, it is also broader in its explanatory power because there are additional reasons for thinking that it is related to conflict-regulating behavior and outcomes. Second, the hypothesis' explanatory power is not great enough to obviate its semiautological weakness. To circumvent this problem the explanatory variable could be reformulated to make it less tautological, or one could try to generalize about the conditions which are likely to engender such attitudes. Both might be possible, but given the hypothesis' functional equivalence to one that has already been offered as a necessary condition, neither is warranted.

Lijphart also states that nonelite attitudes toward the nation serve as a facilitating condition: "National attachments may offset somewhat the unstabilizing effects of deep social cleavages." However, a "very strong nationalism" is not conducive to con-

[91]

flict regulation; it may in fact exacerbate the conflict if super-patriots attribute their nation's weakness to domestic enemies. It is thus only "moderate nationalism" which facilitates conflict regulation.[6] Questions can be raised about both parts of the generalization.

The difficulty with the statement that "a very strong nationalism. . .may become a divisive force and a serious danger to an already fragmented society," is partly semantic. If nationalism refers to a national identity, which I previously defined as the presence of greater loyalties to national symbols, values, and elites than to segmental ones, the statement is clearly false. A strong national identity would promote conflict regulation. If nationalism is taken to mean the kind of diffuse patriotism found in the saying "my nation right or wrong," then the statement does enjoy some validity. Lijphart implicitly moves back and forth between the two definitions. When generalizing about nationalism as a facilitating condition he is apparently thinking of a national identity; when referring to nationalism's exacerbating consequences he is implicitly thinking of its patriotic dimension. He cannot have it both ways. And since his main point relates to the unifying impact of nationalism, we will limit ourselves to a definition of nationalism *qua* national identity.

When we rely upon this meaning of the term nationalism, two problems arise. For one thing, we have already noted that a strong national identity is not found in deeply divided societies, with their powerful segmental attachments and hostilities. If the explanatory variable is at most rarely present in our universe it cannot be used to explain the outcomes of intense conflicts. And, second, while a "moderate" national identity may be found in some deeply divided societies, it will not be strong enough to overcome their powerful centrifugal tendencies. In fact, as far as I can tell, no student of the six countries with which I have been dealing has even characterized the very moderate national feelings in these societies as significant for the regulation of their intense conflicts. Furthermore, the inadequacy of Lijphart's reliance on "moderate nationalism" becomes apparent in his own selection of Belgium and Austria as supporting examples. For it has been said that national sentiment in Belgium is weaker than in any other European country, and a 1956 Austrian survey showed that less than half the population even thought that there is such an entity as an Austrian nation.[7] If national sentiment is

[92]

so weak in Belgium, and if more than half the Austrians do not even believe that an Austrian nation exists, the number of Belgians and Austrians who have any *strong* sentiment for, or who feel any loyalties to, their nations must be quite small. It is difficult to believe that this kind of "moderate nationalism" is anywhere near strong or extensive enough to begin to overcome the powerful centrifugal forces of segmental loyalties and hostilities.

The Crosspressures Hypothesis

The hypothesis that politically relevant divisions which cross-cut each other contribute to the mitigation and regulation of conflicts is probably the explanatory hypothesis most widely accepted among American political scientists.[8] In his first statement of the proposition Georg Simmel reasoned that the criss-crossing of antagonistic groups "serves to 'sew the social system together' by cancelling each other out, thus prevent[ing] disintegration along one primary line of cleavage."[9] Although social scientists differ in their formulations of the independent and dependent variables, all would apply the crosscutting label when a significant proportion of nonelite individuals share two or more politically inconsistent or contradictory differences. These differences may refer to status positions, class and communal differences, preferences for politically relevant goals, affiliations with politically involved associations, party loyalties, or to membership in conflict groups and organizations as defined here.

The major variant of the crosscutting hypothesis suggests that when there is a contradiction between two or more such politically relevant differences, individuals will experience significant crosspressures. The resulting indecision, uncertainty, and psychic strain will lead such individuals to moderate or to drop one or both politically relevant roles, or to attribute less importance to one or both political issues. When this happens among a large number of nonelite individuals the upshot is greater political calm, as crosspressures reduce the total political activity, the total importance attributed to political goals, and the total political affect. Clearly if this reasoning is valid and applicable to divided societies, we would expect a reduction in conflict intensity, concomitantly lessening the likelihood of violent outbursts and making it easier for conflict-regulating practices to be successfully implemented. The reverse statement has also been advanced: reinforcing or superimposing divisions heighten political involvement and increase the intensity with which political values are held, thereby exacerbating the conflict; and by making the conflict even more intractable, they reduce the likelihood of conflict regulation. Thus, out of the conflict itself as it is structured at the nonelite level comes the success or failure of conflict regulation.

Lipset argues that when a significant proportion of the population is pulled by conflicting forces, "its members have an interest in reducing the intensity of political conflict. . . .Multiple and potentially inconsistent affiliations, loyalties, and stimuli reduce the emotion and aggressiveness of political choice." He goes on to relate this generalization to democratic stability. "A stable democracy requires a situation in which all the major political parties include supporters from many segments of the population. A system in which the support of different parties corresponds too closely to basic social divisions cannot continue on a democratic basis, for it reflects a state of conflict so intense and clear-cut as to rule out compromise." [10] Thus, crosscutting differences soften conflicts and facilitate their regulation, while superimposed (or mutually reinforcing) differences aggravate conflicts and severely hinder their regulation.

The underlying rationale of this hypothesis appears eminently plausible. Yet the evidence is too limited, too weak and indirect, to warrant acceptance of the hypothesis as a valid generalization in a theory of conflict regulation.

Much of the supporting evidence for the hypothesis comes from American studies of voting behavior. These studies indicate that electors who experience cross-pressures because of conflict memberships tend to react in the following ways: they lose interest in the campaign, they make their voting decisions later in the campaign, they alter their voting intentions, they experience a reduced feeling of partisanship, if they vote, they split their votes, or they do not vote at all. However, it should be noted that the relationships are mild. The percentage differences between respondents who are and are not crosspressured in their behavior and attitudes are not especially significant, especially given the hypothesis' general acceptance. Moreover, the voting studies only bear out the hypothesis partially and indirectly since they do not include any measures of partisan emotionalism or hostility. Thus, the generalization seems to be valid when voting behavior is taken as the dependent variable, but it does not necessarily explain those attitudes and behaviors which relate to the intensity of conflict. Then, too, findings from the American political *milieu* in the 1950s are not necessarily generalizable to societies experiencing far more severe conflicts. It was perhaps with these last two considerations in mind that Verba attempted to test the hypothesis in the United States and Italy, using the Almond and Verba survey data which include some measures of political hostility. Unfortunately his data were incomplete with respect to the explanatory variable. There was no way of telling whether the American and Italian respondents belonged to the kind of secondary groups which set up crosspressures. Verba therefore had to *assume* that American group members were crosspressured and Italian group members were not. Even then, Verba's sophisticated analysis of the survey data allowed him to conclude only that the hypothesis was not disconfirmed.[12]

The hypothesis has survived what is probably its first direct test in Powell's theoretically guided study of a small Austrian industrial city. Using two survey questions from the Almond and Verba study to get at the respondents' attitudes of political hostility, Powell's data indicate that:

> Lower-class nonclerical Socialist partisans will show more displeasure over the prospect of an OeVP marriage, and will be more likely to fear that the OeVP will endanger the nation, than other Socialist identifiers; upper-class, churchgoing Catholic OeVP identifiers will show more displeasure over a cross-party marriage, will be more likely to fear that the Socialists would endanger the nation, than other OeVP identiers.[13]

However, I would not go so far as to claim, as Powell does, that the data "unambiguously confirm the hypothesis." They support the hypothesis but third variables such as class have not been controlled for and the percentage differences are not large enough, certainly not in a sample of 213 respondents, to warrant such a claim. For example, 9 per cent of those Socialists who were not crosspressured objected to a son or daughter of theirs marrying a supporter of the People's Party, compared to 4 per cent of the Socialists presumably experiencing crosspressures. This small 5 per cent difference does increase to 12, 13, and 17 per cent in the three other crucial comparisons, but the evidence is nevertheless by no means especially persuasive.

The first point to be made about the crosspressures hypothesis is simply this: despite its plausibility, its widespread acceptance is not warranted by the available evidence, which is thin.

There are other, more important doubts to be raised about the hypothesis. It suffers from two omissions which must be remedied. Otherwise even its underlying rationale, and thus plausibility, are in doubt. If crosscutting differences are to engender feelings of being crosspressured, they must be *equally salient and simultaneously experienced*. The critical nature of these two additions is underscored by taking note of the common ability of nonelite individuals to carry around with them highly unstructured and often inconsistent belief systems.[14] Individuals who do not simultaneously experience contradictory loyalties, values, or commitments will therefore not feel crosspressured. They could remain strongly attached to contradictory values and remain active in their pursuit provided the relevant issues were experienced *seriatim* rather than simultaneously.

In their thoughtful analysis of the relationship between communalism and modernization, Melson and Wolpe wrote:

> Since the various identities of any given individual are each "triggered" by different social situations, seemingly incompatible or conflicting identities may well co-exist within the same person. Social roles may, in effect, be "compartmentalized," thereby permitting the individual to respond flexibly to changing social and political circumstances. Thus, it is possible for the same person to join a trade union to advance his occupational interests, a communal association to promote his social or electoral objectives, and a religious interest group to lobby for educational reforms. In short, it is possible for an individual to be both a communal and a non-communal actor.[15]

Melson and Wolpe go on to illustrate this point by noting that Nigerian workers were able to carry out two successful general strikes; they mobilized a class following around the issue of wages. But the trade union leaders failed to convert their following into electoral support for labor candidates in the 1964 election because at that time communal issues "triggered" the workers' regional-tribal loyalties.

> The same trade union leaders who had enjoyed the support of a communally heterogeneous rank-and-file during the 1964 general strike [only a few months before] were deserted when they subsequently transformed themselves from leaders of a socio-economic protest into parliamentary candidates in opposition to the communally-based

regional parties. The moment the strike was concluded, the lines of political cleavage within the nation were redrawn, socio-economic identities once again being subordinated to the communal identities.[16]

Thus despite the political inconsistency between the Nigerian workers' class and tribal connections they could pursue both sets of interests and values intensely and without experiencing any crosspressures since the two issues came to the political forefront at different times. The nonsimultaneous appearance of politically inconsistent differences allows individuals to compartmentalize contradictory attitudes without experiencing any significant crosspressures. There are other ways in which compartmentalization may occur, with or without psychological strain, but these are culturally and psychologically too diverse to include in the hypothesis. However, simultaneity is an indispensable condition.

In addition, politically relevant differences must be almost equally salient for the individuals if they are to set up the kinds of crosspressures that help mitigate conflicts. An individual who values or feels loyal to both X and Y, but who places a far greater value upon X, will probably not experience significant crosspressures, thus being able to pursue X with unchanging intensity even when Y is present. Returning to the Nigerian example, it is clear that regional-tribal loyalties were far more salient and intensely felt than were class interests and identities. It was this differential salience rather than crosspressures (which were absent) that explains the workers' positive response to their tribal parties, while rejecting electoral appeals for a labor party that would bring together members of the major communal segments.[17] Which is to say that without nearly equal salience conflict intensities are not reduced since crosspressures are absent or mildly experienced at best.

This point is generally relevant in those communally divided societies in which class divisions cut across communal ones. In the great majority of communally divided societies members of the same conflict groups do belong to different classes, but since their attachments tend to differ markedly in their salience, the individuals are not usually subjected to crosspressures. The historical and contemporary record indicates that in societies which are deeply divided along communal lines, whether these be religious, racial, tribal, linguistic or ethnic lines, crosscutting class identities and interests are rarely of equal salience. The objectively defined crosscutting pattern is not sufficiently forceful

[97]

on a subjective level to engender significantly felt crosspressures. Pre-1917 Holland constitutes one of the few exceptions. Cross-cutting class and religious divisions were then of almost equally high salience.

The far more common pattern is exemplified by Northern Ireland. During the last fifty years religious divisions have been much more salient than class divisions, and this despite Ulster's industrialization which "should have" activated class conflict. In a recent survey, Ulster respondents were asked whether they identify with their class, religion, nationality and party. Almost four times as many identified with their religion as with their class (42 per cent versus 12 per cent). If nationality and party are taken as indirect indicators of religious identification—in Northern Ireland's politics there is a good deal of perceived overlap among them—eight times as many respondents identified with their religion as with their class.[18] In Malaysia, Chinese and Malay farmers growing the same crop in the same district will have no communication and perceive themselves as having nothing in common except the institutions imposed upon them by the regime.[19] With regard to nonwestern societies in general, Anderson et al. maintain that "race, language and religion especially are capable of generating an intensity of identification which can eclipse all other issues—or absorb other conflicts and translate them into communal hostility."[20] They go on to indicate why communal attachments are of such a high salience that they can easily subsume other divisions, such as class divisions.

> Racial consciousness, facilitated by its extreme visibility, creates its own stereotypes of cultural differentiation. Language, as the medium of social communication, simultaneously creates networks of intensive social communications. . . .Religion, by positing a divine or supernatural imperative for communal identity, removes differentiation from the plane of human rationality or debate. Conflict can become invested with a mandate from heaven and be pursued as a holy duty.[21]

Other reasons could readily be added. Yet it should be clear without doing so that class loyalties and values infrequently generate the same intensity of attachment as communal ones when they crosscut each other—or more specifically, when they "compete with each other." Class divisions will thus regularly be significantly less salient, obviating subjectively felt crosspressures.

These comments severely call the hypothesis' validity into question. At a minimum, it needs to be reformulated so as to

[98]

deal with these two omissions. This could certainly be done, but then the hypothesis would come up against quite a different problem. When the requirements that contradictory values be of nearly equal salience and almost simultaneously triggered are added, the hypothesis gains in plausibility but loses in scope of applicability. In fact, there may be very few societies in which these and other aspects of the explanatory variable are found together. Yet this problem would not be crucial were it not that the hypothesis' scope is reduced practically to the vanishing point when applied to deeply divided societies.

Even if it were somehow possible to ignore the two additional requirements, the hypothesis is not useful as a general explanation because it is applicable to too small a proportion of deeply divided societies. Such societies contain very few crosscutting loyalties, values, issues or group memberships; politically relevant attachments almost always form a mutually reinforcing pattern. The segments, conflict groups, conflict organizations and divisive issues are securely and quite rigidly superimposed on one another. Intense conflicts often feature two, three, or four major issues. But in the great majority of instances multiple issues do not form crosscutting patterns and do not set up crosspressures. They are politically compatible because the same segments, conflict groups, and conflict organizations oppose each other on every issue. For example, the Malay and Chinese conflict groups and their respective conflict organizations (UMNO and MCA) divided consistently not only over the official language question, but over issues of state support for religious institutions, the state's symbolic paraphernalia, citizenship rights for the Chinese and numerous specific distributive issues. The Austrian conflict groups (the two *Lager*) opposed each other over religious questions, economic redistribution, and the government's economic control and ownership. The Protestants and Catholics in nineteenth-century Switzerland consistently opposed each other on religious questions, the federation's structure, and the government's economic policies. In short, in deeply divided societies issue positions are not seen to be incompatible, and group attachments are mutually reinforcing. Individuals are thus most unlikely to find themselves being crosspressured. This finding severely limits the hypothesis' applicability, and thus its usefulness for our purposes.

A final point questions the hypothesis' presumed validity

[99]

at the macro-level. It has been suggested that superimposed political differences necessarily obviate the possibility of democratic stability, and thus conflict regulation as defined here. Yet in mid-nineteenth-century Switzerland, early twentieth-century Belgium, and in contemporary Austria, Lebanon, and Malaysia intense conflicts have been regulated in the presence of superimposed divisions. A less ambitious but still very important claim is made for the hypothesis when it is advanced as a fairly strong tendency statement in explaining conflict-regulating outcomes. We have not examined a large enough number of cases to assess the validity of this claim on the basis of numerical evidence, but one aspect of our previous discussion—the point that very few deeply divided societies exhibit a forceful crosscutting pattern—does call it into question. If there is so little variation in the presence or absence of the independent variable, we would be hard pressed to use it in explaining extensive variations in the dependent variable. If the great majority of intense conflicts are structured according to the superimposition pattern, the latter cannot be generally used to account for the not infrequent instances of successful conflict regulation.

There are thus four reasons for not using the crosspressures hypothesis to explain conflict regulation: 1) it is not especially plausible, given the limited, weak, and indirect supporting evidence; 2) two necessary conditions—the nearly equal salience of crosscutting divisions and their simultaneous triggering—have been omitted from the explanatory variable, and, if included, they would drastically restrict the hypothesis' applicability; 3) since the vast majority of deeply divided societies manifest only the mutually reinforcing pattern the hypothesis' applicability is further restricted in its applicability to the regulation of severe conflicts; and 4) there is reason to doubt the presence of a correlation between crosscutting divisions and successful conflict regulation.

On the other hand, the hypothesis is supported by too much evidence, and enjoys too persuasive a socio-psychological rationale, for it to be discarded completely. I would suggest that it remains highly plausible in accounting for two phenomena. Despite the criticisms levelled at the hypothesis, the crosscutting pattern can probably go a long way in accounting for the manner and effectiveness with which mild and only moderately sharp conflicts are handled. More important for future work on conflict and conflict regulation, the hypothesis might be very useful

[100]

in explaining why some conflicts become severe and others do not. A pattern of mutually reinforcing divisions could account for the transformation of mild conflicts into intense conflicts. Considering that the great majority of intense conflicts are structured according to the superimposition pattern, it may very well be that it is just this pattern which helps intensify the conflicts to begin with. Which is to say that regulatory outcomes have occurred despite the superimposition pattern, leading us to look elsewhere for those factors which can explain the regulation of conflicts once they have become intense.

The Crosscutting Divisions Hypothesis

In assessing the validity and applicability of the crosspressures hypothesis we have referred exclusively to its major variant, which focuses upon the individual or micro-level. There is a second, less well known variant, which also focuses on crosscutting differences, but does not rely on crosspressures. It relates crosscutting differences to the electoral strategies of party leaders, and then to conflict regulation. When two or more political issues are present which are themselves crosscutting or cut across party attachments, party leaders tend to play down one or another in order to attract additional supporters—potential supporters who would not vote for the party if it adamantly pursued issues X and Y, but who might very well do so if the Y issue were played down or dropped. For example, in setting out the conditions that account for Belgium's political stability in the midst of the Fleming-Walloon conflict, Lorwin takes note of three politically relevant factors—religion, class, and party loyalties—which cut across the regional-language conflict, and thereby provide a good measure of "national cohesion." Although secondary [party] leaders defend chiefly Flemish or Walloon or Brussels interests, the top [party] leaders "are highly conscious of their role in the aggregation of regional claims. . . .In their own interests they work to surmount the tendencies toward further polarization (along regional-linguistic lines)." [22] And I previously noted that in the late 1950s the Belgian Liberals dropped their one-hundred-and-thirty-year-old anticlericalism in order to appeal to middle-class Catholics. In this manner crosscutting differences of the nonelite level may facilitate the party leaders' regulatory efforts.

I do not, however, view this hypothesis as particularly useful in accounting for conflict-regulating outcomes. For one thing, party leaders would be facing an extremely difficult and thus problematic task in attempting to win over additional supporters. Even in the presense of crosscutting divisions individuals on one side of the conflict line (in terms of their voting behavior and partisan beliefs) will not cross that line just because party leaders play down one issue and emphasize another. Social constraints, hostile feelings, negative beliefs and distrust are too many and too strong to be overcome by an appeal on one conflict issue. Recognizing these usually insuperable roadblocks, party leaders have commonly attempted to increase their electoral strength by attempting to politicize and mobilize additional supporters within their own segments. In Austria, for example, with the exceptional importance attributed to electoral outcomes in revising the distribution of governmental power during the Grand Coalition, the party leaders opted for a strategy of further politicization rather than of appealing across class divisions by altering their positions on religious or economic issues. "The easiest and safest way of achieving incremental gains and avoiding incremental losses at the polls was to be simply more efficient in mobilizing 'your' *Lager* than your opponent was in mobilizing 'his' *Lager*." [23] According to Rose, "if politics in Northern Ireland divided people along class lines, then Protestants and Catholics currently in different parties might come together in parties as familiar and peaceable as those prevailing in Britain. A wide variety of politicians have sought to introduce such a transformation, from the time of James Connolly to the Prime Ministership of Terence O'Neil." All have failed. [24]

Furthermore, trying to enlarge partisan support by appealing across segmental lines is a risky business for the party leaders. Such an appeal is sure to alienate some conflict group members and leaders. Even if it succeeds, the not uncommon outcome is party fragmentation. It may be significant that among Western European parties, those in Northern Ireland are the least cohesive. Considering the risks involved as well as the likelihood of failure because of the difficulties to be overcome, party leaders in divided societies rarely behave in the manner suggested by the hypothesis. Moreover, even if the leaders discounted the risks and difficulties involved, their attempts to appeal across segmental lines are just as likely (if not more so) to produce party fragmentation than the aggregation (and thus the conciliation)

[102]

of diverse interests within more inclusive parties. The likelihood of this outcome is even further increased in the presence of cross-cutting divisions. Weimar Germany, France, and Italy, with their numerous, uncohesive and "anti-system" parties, are cases in point.

At a minimum, one other condition would have to be satisfied if party leaders are to behave according to the hypothesis' dictates. Dahl would maintain that this additional condition is to be found in the differential salience of the crosscutting issues. Only then will they facilitate conciliation rather than party fragmentation. "Unifying effects cannot occur if all the cleavages are felt with equal intensity. Conciliation is encouraged by cross-cutting cleavages *only* if some cleavages are less significant than others." [25] Only when the issues are unequally salient would the party leaders yield on the less salient ones in order to pursue the salient ones more effectively by attracting potential (and diverse) supporters. Dahl is correct in suggesting that these less salient issues would consequently be easier to regulate and resolve once most of the major political parties enjoyed the support of some nonelite individuals who take similar positions on these issues. However, it does not follow that crosscutting divisions plus unequal salience of the corresponding issues will generally contribute to conflict regulation. Even if party leaders were to mitigate their positions on the less salient issues, members of the opposing conflict group are not likely to change their party attachments on the basis of a secondary issue. Indeed, this point constitutes an additional reason for thinking that party leaders will fail in their efforts, as they have in Northern Ireland, where the appeal across religious lines to the far less salient class issue has been ignored. Moreover, even if this last point is not accepted, the successful conciliation of secondary issues would probably contribute little to regulatory outcomes. For it is the most salient divisions and the corresponding issues which structure the conflict's intensity, and until these are dealt with effectively regulatory outcomes remain problematic.

A final reason for not accepting this variant of the cross-cutting hypothesis as an explanation for conflict regulation has already been mentioned. There are very few intensely divided societies which feature the cross-cutting pattern at the nonelite level. If party leaders rarely have the opportunity to attract a diverse following and thereby presumably contribute to the conflict's regulation the hypothesis can hardly be offered as a general explanation. Besides post-1945 Belgium, the only other relevant instance that I know of is pre-World War I Holland, where religious and class differences intersected. The confessional parties presumably wanted the support of the soon-to-be enfranchised workers over and above the middle-class support which they already enjoyed. Toward this goal they may have regulated the class conflict in order to attain the support of Protestant and Catholic workers whose enfranchisement was part of the national compromise of 1917. Unfortunately there is no adequate discussion of party strategies and motivations during this period. This second example of crosscutting differences as they facilitate the regulation of intense conflicts must therefore remain only a possibility.

For these reasons I would not want to rely upon this variant of the crosscutting hypothesis in trying to account for conflict regulation. Yet there is a point to the hypothesis, and it is applicable to the regulation of one or two of our intense conflicts. Rather than omit the hypothesis it might be integrated into another part of the study as a subsidiary proposition. The hypothesis is built upon the implicit assumption that party leaders are motivated to dampen certain issues in order to acquire governmental offices and power. But instead of accepting the hypothesis' implicit claim that party leaders are *generally* willing and able to dampen issues in the presence of a crosscutting pattern, we may say that one factor which may allow leaders to increase their political power is the simultaneous presence and unequal salience of crosscutting issues at the nonelite level. Thus, though the latter do not generally or directly facilitate conflict regulation, they may occasionally do so in an indirect manner when party leaders possess the relevant motivations and are able to act upon them.

Segmental Isolation

One conclusion drawn from our discussion of the crosscutting hypothesis' major variant suggests that intense conflicts have been regulated *despite* the superimposition pattern. Or, to put it differently, crosscutting divisions cannot account for conflict-regulating outcomes; these have sometimes occurred in the face of those mutually reinforcing divisions which contributed

[104]

to the conflicts' original intensification. There is another possibility which deserves serious consideration: regulatory outcomes have occurred *because* of mutually reinforcing divisions. This possibility is related to Lijphart's most important explanation of regulatory outcomes: the isolation of opposing segments, or what he calls "distinct lines of cleavage between subcultures."[26] The two statements overlap extensively with regard to spatial patterns. One type of mutually reinforcing division is a territorial one, which is often imposed upon linguistic, tribal and racial divisions. When territorial divisions correspond to one of these communal divisions, opposing communal segments are also spatially isolated from each other within the same society. In Lijphart's hypothesis the distinct separation between segments (what he calls subcultures) is not limited to spatial patterns. Equally important are the minimization of intersegmental contacts on the job, in the schools, and over the mass communications network.

The reasoning behind the hypothesis begins with the point that segmental isolation will make it patently clear to the elites that disintegrative dangers are lurking just around the corner. "Indeed, the more extreme the condition of cleavage and mutual isolation, the clearer the danger signals are likely to be perceived. Once the peril is recognized, remedies may be applied."[27] In conjunction with other factors, this clear-cut awareness brought about by segmental isolation presumably increases the likelihood of a "positive response" on the part of elites. While the reasoning is eminently sound, it is not (at least for our present purposes) especially significant. In the context of an intense conflict, despite extensive intersegmental contacts, conflict group leaders are usually well aware of the potential for violence and instability. And where the leaders are unaware of this potential it is probably because the intensity has not (yet) given rise to widespread demonstrations, riots, or individual acts of violence, and not because of segmental isolation. Lijphart's second point is more persuasive. It links up with the previously stated importance of structured elite predominance. Segmental isolation is said to be propitious for maintaining the cohesion of conflict groups, and thus the ability of the leaders to predominate over their followers.[28] Spatial propinquity of conflict group members and their exclusive social and economic contacts facilitate conflict group cohesion, and thus elite predominance.

The third point is the most persuasive. The probability that conflict group antagonisms will be acted out in a violent fashion are sharply reduced when the number of intersegmental contacts at the nonelite level is minimal. When the "enemy" is out of sight it is not out of mind, but nonelites are far less capable of making a direct and negative conflict-regulating "contribution"— an important point supported by related generalizations advanced by Coser and Deutsch among others.[29] The absence of opportunities to give violent expression to their antagonisms also facilitates elite attempts to work out, implement, and maintain conflict-regulating practices. The hypothesis' plausibility is enhanced when we note the extensive degree of segmental isolation found in nineteenth-century Switzerland, and contemporary Lebanon and Malaysia. Within contemporary Belgium, the Fleming-Francophone conflict has been most intensely experienced in Brussels' linguistically mixed environs. And in Malaysia, the two major race riots broke out in cities where the Malays and Chinese were not spatially isolated. I would go on to suggest that Lijphart's third point in support of the segmental isolation hypothesis has a special applicability to what are called "contested areas"— areas gradually being populated by members of one segment which had previously been dominated by another segment. For example, the 1958 Ceylon riots began next to a Tamil population center where Sinhalese colonists had recently been settled. In Guyana, many of the worst incidents took place in established Negro villages into which Indians had later moved. Lijphart's point is also particularly applicable to areas featuring a striking imbalance in the size of contiguous segmental populations. In these areas there is a very real danger that the locally predominant segment (or its conflict group members) will terrorize the minority, as happened between Hindus and Moslems during partition, in the 1956 race riots between the Sinhalese and Tamils in those areas of Ceylon in which the former predominated, and, recently, between the Protestant majority and Catholic minority in the major cities of Northern Ireland.

The hypothesis' rationale is thus not only eminently sensible, a large handful of supporting examples further enhance its plausibility. But before it can be accepted as an explanation of conflict regulation a counterargument must be confronted. It is sometimes alleged that intersegmental contacts breed greater mutual tolerance and trust, even mutual understanding and empathy. I am referring to the kind of argument heard in the United States, in which it is maintained that a movement out of the Black ghettoes would soften racial tensions as the segments interacted in residential districts, in schools, and on the job. Social scientists are aware of the general tendency for people to confrom or over-conform to group norms. When group norms entail hostility to opposing groups, as in deeply divided societies, there is reason to believe that segmental isolation breeds and maintains inter-segmental hostility. Evidence for the counterargument comes from Malaysia, Holland and Northern Ireland.

According to a close student of Malaysian politics the past isolation of Malays and Chinese has contributed to conflict regulation, but what is needed now is intersegmental communica-tion at all levels, not just within the executive of the intercom-munal Alliance. Increased communication will not guarantee the conflict's regulation, but "without dialogue. . .the lines of conflict will become even more rigid." [30] The segmentation of radio and television programs, with separate wave lengths for each of the three segments, has been most extensively realized in contemporary Holland. While I do not place the Netherlands of the 1960s on my list of intensely divided societies, Lorwin's comment is relevant to the general point. "It was futile to expect most people not to watch programs indiscriminately. Although programs have occasionally shocked viewers of other blocs (i.e., segments), the general effect on the masses, who did not normally share social life with members of other blocs, has been to weaken old stereotypes and enhance understanding of other groups. Since television programs brought intrabloc as well as interbloc con-flicts into the living rooms of the ordinarily deferential Dutch citizens, they also had some effect on the simplified self-images of the segmented society." [31] In a recent survey conducted in Northern Ireland the respondents were ranked according to the proportion of Protestant or Catholic co-religionists with whom they had social relations. Among Protestants the number of re-spondents who took "Ultra" positions asserting their readiness to defy basic political laws rises from 28 per cent in the least socially segregated group to 64 per cent in the most segregated. The percentages for Catholic respondents increase less markedly, from 39 percent to 50 per cent. The data also ironically imply that "the best way to reduce violent anti-regime views is to place Protestants in a predominantly Catholic environment." Given population ratios this type of mixing is impossible on a large scale in Northern Ireland, even if some courageously foolhardy politicians were to push for it.[32]

How then is the validity of Lijphart's hypothesis to be evaluated in light of this counterargument? Since the notion of segmental isolation is so broad and multifaceted, it would seem sensible to break it down into its component parts. Once this is done it will be easier to assess its validity by looking at the consequences of different types of isolation. We can differentiate, at least in gross terms, between spatial isolation of segments and their socio-cultural isolation or what may be called their encapsulation. People are spatially isolated according to where they live and work; encapsulation refers to where people send their children to school, whom they socialize with, and where they turn in the mass communications spectrum. The significance of this differentiation lies in the fact that people have very little choice in deciding where to live and work; they are heavily constrained by their desire to live near relatives and old friends, where their occupations may best be pursued, and where they feel safest in the context of an intense conflict. The constraints are far less forceful in deciding where to educate one's children, whom to talk to and see socially, which radio or television program to tune in on, and which newspaper to read. When intersegmental contacts in deeply divided societies are dictated by the constraints of spatial patterns these contacts are infrequently desired and often positively distasteful to one or both segments. They are consequently more likely to intensify hostile feelings and to multiply their behavioral expressions than intersegmental contacts which result from a much freer choice. Under conditions of relatively free choice the "crossing" of segmental lines is less likely to intensify conflict because intersegmental contacts are then desired; at worst, individuals can move back "across" the line.

I am not arguing that segmental encapsulation—that is, largely unconstrained intersegmental contacts of a socio-cultural variety—tends to facilitate conflict regulation by promoting mutual tolerance and perhaps understanding as well. This may or may not be the case; given our contradictory and limited knowledge such a proposition would be exceptionally tenuous. I would argue, however, that at least intersegmental contacts of a largely free-choice variety do not aggravate the conflict or make its regulation significantly more difficult. Encapsulation does contribute somewhat to the structured predominance of elites (the second reason given by Lijphart in support of his hypothesis), but this point is of secondary significance, and it is balanced by the possibility that relatively unconstrained intersegmental contacts actually promote tolerance and understanding between segments. This leads me to the conclusion that Lijphart's hypothesis should be restricted to segmental isolation in the spatial sense, dropping socio-cultural encapsulation from the generalization.

On the other hand, if the hypothesis is limited to spatial isolation, other difficulties arise when we introduce a distinction between two types of spatial isolation. Territorial isolation refers to a broad concentration of segments within large geographical areas; territorial isolation exists when the opposing segments live in different regions of the country, or when we speak of a country as segmentally divided along a North-South or East-West axis. Areal isolation (for want of a better term) refers to spatial isolation on a much smaller geographical scale, with different segments living and working in different parts of the same area, whether this be a city, its outlying areas, a cluster of towns, or a single province. Within these areas segments are concentrated within different neighborhoods, sections, locales or towns.

With regard to territorial isolation, the hypothesis now faces two difficulties. Territorial isolation need not necessarily entail inequalities in wealth, status, power and other values; it may simply involve geographical isolation and some autonomy in the cultural and social spheres. Yet the two usually go hand in hand, and as such, they make for the conflict's exacerbation rather than regulation. "In the modern world. . .segregation (i.e., territorial isolation) has meant more than just cultural and social autonomy; it has meant also unequal access to education, to the economy, and to political power. It is by maintaining and promoting such inequalities that segregation has promoted communal conflict." [33] Moreover, territorial isolation increases the probability of the most violent form of strife—civil war. The strong identification of one segment and its values with the territory it inhabits may readily produce demands for some form of semiautonomy, and its concentration of population and power within the territory heightens the readiness of both leaders and followers to escalate demands if their original ones are not met.[34] There is a well trod path from territorial isolation, to demands for semiautonomy, to separatist goals, their rejection by the centralist-oriented con-

[109]

flict group, to a bloody civil war or the forceful repression of the separatist segment by the centralist-minded conflict group. Massive violence and/or forceful repression in the Congo, Nigeria, the Sudan, Ireland circa World War I, the United States in the nineteenth century, and in much of Eastern Europe during the interwar period dramatically attest to the reality of this possibility.

Thus, despite the good reasons offered by Lijphart for thinking that territorial isolation promotes conflict regulation, on balance it would seem that territorial isolation does not generally facilitate conflict regulation. Indeed, territorial isolation may even negate conflict-regulating outcomes, especially when the separatist-minded segment adjoins an international border. For all these reasons I would like to leave territorial isolation an open question and not include it in my hypotheses.

The original hypothesis has now been reduced to areal isolation. Yet here too there is a crucial difficulty. The hypothesis that areal isolation promotes conflict regulation could only hold true if there is a good deal of variation in this type of isolation; only if such variation exists can we even hope to find an association between areal isolation and conflict-regulating outcomes. Yet areal isolation with class and communal segments clustering together in different neighborhoods, locales, sections or towns, is to a very large extent present in the great majority of societies. More to the point, it is widely present in *every* deeply divided society where in-group feelings and the desire for security are especially strong. And since a constant (or near constant) cannot explain extensive variation, areal isolation must be rejected as an explanatory variable. Thus despite the seeming plausibility of Lijphart's hypothesis, we have to conclude that segmental isolation of a spatial or socio-cultural variety does not facilitate conflict regulation.

The Impact of Modernization

Our rejection of five seemingly plausible nonelite hypotheses as explanations of conflict regulation raises a broad and intriguing question: are nonelite variables quite irrelevant in accounting for regulatory outcomes? An affirmative reply should leave us somewhat uneasy, since conflict regulation has on occasion failed because of spontaneous violence by the nonelite or its pursuit of

[110]

a violent course in the face of elite objections. The spontaneous violence which involved more than a million deaths in the partition of India and Pakistan, the Hutu slaughter of many thousands of Tutsi in Rwanda circa 1960, the nonelite rioting and violence which touched off a civil war in the Sudan, the hundreds of thousands of deaths in Colombia's *violencia*—these are just a few cases which indicate the presumed importance of using nonelite variables in explaining nonelite behavior. To some extent our theoretical statement has "covered" such cases by the inclusion of structured elite predominance as a necessary condition. Nevertheless, presumably there are other factors which help explain why nonelites make direct and negative "contributions" to conflict regulation in the form of riots, terror, arson, violence and atrocities.

Yet the nonelite hypotheses in the literature do not hold up; nor have I been able to think of any other nonelite characteristics which can form the bases of plausible explanatory hypotheses. At this point we should therefore raise the possibility that nonelite attributes themselves do not help explain regulatory outcomes, but that explanations may be found in certain developments whose impact upon the nonelite may account for their behavior. Certain social, economic, or political factors may have an impact upon the nonelite which may in turn make regulatory outcomes more or less likely. Such a formulation would recognize the importance of nonelite behavior without however relying upon nonelite characteristics to explain that behavior. I would argue that one plausible explanatory is to be found in the process of socio-economic modernization. I would like to develop this explanation, at least in a skeletal fashion. But before doing so, a caveat is in order which indicates why it is appropriate only to sketch the argument at this time.

In chapter I it was said that the regulation of intense conflicts could be studied without first inquiring into those conditions which gave rise to the conflicts' intensity. It is only here, at the end of the study, that this assumption becomes awkward. Socio-economic modernization does have an impact upon nonelites in deeply divided societies which reduces the chances of realizing regulatory outcomes. But modernization is of equal, if not greater importance, in accounting for the emergence of intense conflicts. And as such, it would make good sense to generalize about the impact of modernization upon nonelites as

[111]

it patterns both the intensification of conflict and its regulation. On the other hand, rather than relegating a discussion of modernization to the confines of another and more comprehensive study, the argument can be briefly outlined in the present study. I shall desist from offering examples, evidence, caveats or full statements of the various arguments in support of the following proposition: socio-economic modernization (under conditions to be specified) *detracts* from the realization of regulatory outcomes in societies deeply divided along communal lines by further increasing the number of nonelite individuals who manifest hostile beliefs, feelings and jealousies toward the opposing segment, by further intensifying such attitudes among individuals who already hold them, and by placing individuals in situations which allow or encourage them to act out their antagonistic beliefs and feelings. It should be noted that this particular hypothesis is not applicable to European societies for reasons that will soon become apparent.

1. The first point to be made is one of specification. The argument is applicable to societies in which modernization has had a powerful impact in intensifying conflicts, but since the modernization process is virtually inexorable once underway, continuing modernization during the period of intense conflict will reduce the probability of regulatory outcomes. The argument is also applicable to those societies which have experienced intense conflicts before the onset of modernization. The latter can not then be used to explain the intense conflict's emergence, but it can help account for its regulation. The first type of society approximates Furnivall's model of the "plural society." Plural societies are made up of two or more segments whose institutions, cultures, and values differ fundamentally; there are no overarching bonds, values, or loyalties; the "society" is held together only by the colonial government; contacts between segments are rare, minimal, or limited to economic interactions; and the segments engage in different or separate economic activities.[35] In these societies the modernization process goes a long way in deepening already existing divisions; once the conflict has become intense, the continuing impact of modernization upon the nonelite detracts from the possibility of regulatory outcomes. The second type of society, in which conflict is already intense prior to modernization, approximates the model of a plural society set out by Furnivall's most prominent interpreter and critic. On the basis of his study of the British West Indies, and more recently of tropical

[112]

Africa, Smith added two components to the model. He places greater emphasis than does Furnivall upon the mutual hostility of the segments, over and above their separateness and differences, and maintains that one segment usually dominates the others(s). It is this domination—with the dominant segment holding highly unflattering beliefs about the subordinate segment(s), and the subordinate segment(s) suffering under and resenting the dominant one—which largely accounts for the intensity of segmental hostilities.[36] When nonelites in such societies experience the impact of modernization the likelihood of regulatory outcomes decreases significantly.

2. Modernization has its most deleterious consequences for conflict regulation in divided societies which are just beginning to modernize and are doing so at a relatively rapid rate. New experiences and the rapidity with which they unfold heighten those anxieties, insecurities, and fears stemming from the modernization process itself, concomitantly increasing their impact on intersegmental conflict and violence. The hypothesis thus has its greatest applicability among contemporary nonwestern societies characterized by a combination of open regimes (at least on an intermittent basis since 1945), intense communal conflicts, low levels of modernization, and the activation of the modernization process. The hypothesis is limited to communal conflicts in these societies because intense class conflicts are quite rare in today's communally segmented nonwestern societies; modernization also has a differential upon the two types of conflicts. Despite limitations in space and time, the hypothesis is applicable to a sizeable universe, including Malaysia, Lebanon, Cyprus, the Sudan, Nigeria, Uganda, Zambia, Rwanda, Ceylon, India, Pakistan, Indonesia, Burma and Laos among others.

3. Modernization increases the level of social mobilization, politicization, and political participation. In deeply divided societies this entails an increased ratio of conflict group members to segmental size increases, thereby potentially increasing the frequency of violence, and, when it does break out, enlarging it scope.

4. Modernization helps make men more alike, installing similar values and desires. Men come to value the same economic rewards, creating a competitive situation in contrast to the economic specialization and compartmentalization found in plural societies prior to modernization—a time when communal rioting

[113]

and violence were rarely occasioned by economic rivalries. In communally divided societies this competition for scarce economic rewards is turned into segmental channels as individuals come to rely heavily upon their communal identities and resources in pursuing the economic rewards of modernity. The strenuous competition-conflict for these rewards is especially ruthless in the public sector. It is here that the segments clash most often and most intensely because governmental jobs are far more desirable than others, each segment believes it has a legitimate right to a sizeable (or disproportionate) number of these jobs, and their allocation is readily influenced by more or less peaceful political pressures.

5. Modernization may or may not increase material standards of life. But it certainly increases expectations, and since these can rarely be satisfied, the result is a pervasive sense of relative deprivation. Discontent and frustration often give rise to the anger, hate and rage which is almost invariably present when violence occurs. And in deeply divided societies feelings of relative deprivation are sharply and ineluctably focused upon the opposing segment, even when that segment has been assigned a smaller share of material rewards.

6. Approximately half of the nonwestern societies are linguistically diverse. In this context, modernization further intensifies communal conflicts by first helping to propel language issues into the conflict's limelight. It does so by increasing the number, extent and importance of school and university places, jobs in the modern sector, public employment, urban areas and geographical mobility. The language issue comes to have enormous importance for many people. For a number of reasons, including the fact that linguistic segments also differ along racial, tribal, religious or ethnic lines, the language issue is pursued through opposing conflict groups and organizations.

7. The previously mentioned consequences of modernization not only all come together in the expanding urban areas, but urbanization further escalates the conflict and brings men together spatially so that they can more easily act out their violent urgings. Urban areas provide somewhat more fertile ground for popular activism than does a rural setting. The competition-conflict for material rewards is most fiercely pursued in the cities; men have been pulled or pushed into the cities for just this reason. The competition may occur in almost a face-to-face manner, the

[114]

cities contain the unemployed losers, and there are relatively few means of survival other than a job. In the towns and cities the competition-conflict is almost ineluctably defined in communal terms given the fears and resentments of those who already hold jobs when faced with the influx of segmental outsiders hungry for work, while the newcomers' jealousies, ambitions, and insecurities lead them to the shelter and resources of their own communal compatriots. The struggle for government jobs is also pursued most forcefully in the urban-administrative centers where the jobs exist, and where a politicized population may be used as a means for their attainment. Relative deprivation is often most sharply and extensively experienced in an urban setting; it is here that expectations are highest and contrasts between the haves and have-nots are most glaring and visible. The personal anxieties and frustrations that afflict many men as they experience the impact of modernization are often deflected upon outgroups, rather than being internalized or accepted for what they are, when the outgroups are visible and present. The language conflict is most pervasively and sharply experienced in the cities. Language is part and parcel of the competition-conflict for governmental and private employment which is most viciously pursued in the cities, it is in the national and regional capitals that language issues are decided, it is in the cities that the speakers of different languages compete for scarce economic rewards, and because of segmental intermingling it is here that slurs upon a man's language are most often (inadvertently or purposefully) made. And finally, all the hostile feelings of jealousy, bitterness, fear, animosity and hatred that are related to the onset of modernization in communally divided societies can most readily be acted out in an urban setting where the hostile segments are visible, proximate, and in contact with each other.

There are undoubtedly social, economic and political developments other than the modernization process whose impact upon the nonelite heightens or lowers the probability of regulatory outcomes. The nonelite's exceptionally rapid enfranchisement is one such possibility. Among other reasons for thinking this to be a plausible hypothesis, the practically overnight introduction of universal suffrage tends to stimulate real or imaginary fears within the minority conflict group—fears of being politically overwhelmed and dominated by the larger conflict group, resulting in strenuous opposition to the majoritarian institutions, and

[115]

then a resort to violence or governmental repression to win a struggle that cannot be won at the ballot box. The unsuccessful regulation of intense class conflicts in Italy, Austria and Germany follows this pattern.[37] But as is true of the modernization variable, the rapid expansion of the electorate is also closely related to the conflicts' original intensification. Indeed, it may very well be that all those factors which impinge upon the nonelites in deeply divided societies are equally, or more, important, in accounting for the emergence of intense conflicts to begin with. We must reserve any further generalizations along these lines for another study.

VII

A Summary and Some Future Directions

The theory developed here is a literal one in the sense that it consists of a number of general propositions, descriptive generalizations, and explanatory hypotheses standing at different levels of explanation. Some of them bear on the dependent variable directly while some relate to each other in the form of an integrated and coherent theoretical statement. Given the complexity of the hypothesized inter-relationships it would seem useful to summarize the study's conclusions by setting out the various propositions. Such a summary may also prove useful in suggesting additional relationships (and perhaps highlighting contradictions) among the hypotheses. It will certainly be of some use in assessing the theory's overall plausibility and in subjecting it to empirical tests.

1. When intense conflicts are successfully regulated one, or more, of six conflict-regulating practices is always employed. The six practices are the stable coalition, the proportionality principle, depoliticization, the mutual veto, compromise and concessions.

2. An exclusive reliance upon majoritarian institutions and practices does not facilitate conflict regulation, and may even contribute to conflict exacerbation.

3. Efforts to regulate conflict by creating a national identity in a short period of time will not only be unsuccessful, they will more than likely lead to widespread violence and governmental repression.

[117]

4. Conflict group leaders play a critical role in the process of conflict regulation. They, and they alone, can make a direct and positive contribution. As for conflict group members, their impact on regulatory outcomes can only be directly negative or indirectly positive or negative.

5. Conflict-regulating motives are a necessary condition if elites are to engage in conflict-regulating behavior. More specifically, one or more of four motivations must be present if elites are to make regulatory efforts: the strong desire to ward off pressure from external states, to maintain or increase the level of economic well being, to acquire or retain governmental offices and power, or to avoid bloodshed among the leaders' own segment.

6. These motivations are most likely to appear under certain conditions: the desire to fend off external demands is most often found among countries at the lower end of the international power ladder; economic motives are most strongly felt and expressed in the presence of a sizeable commercial class dedicated to the pursuit of economic values; the desire for governmental office and power is most likely where no conflict group forms a majority or expects to do so in the forseeable future; and the strife-avoidance goal is most likely to be highly valued when elites believe in the very real possibility of civil strife, this perception being most frequent in societies that have already suffered from major civil strife or are experiencing rioting and sporadic violence.

7. Conflict-group leaders who adhere to conciliatory attitudes tend to engage in regulatory efforts far more readily than leaders who do not. When these attitudes are present, it is much more probable that regulatory efforts will be translated into regulatory practices.

8. The emergence of conciliatory attitudes among elites may be explained by a psycho-historical model of attitude formation requiring repetitive and regularly rewarded conciliatory behavior. This model generated specific hypotheses in which the long-term presence of any one of the four motivations mentioned in paragraph 5 above, which is in turn dependent upon the presence of the four conditions mentioned in paragraph 6 above, contributes to the formation of conciliatory attitudes. Once formed, these attitudes are transmitted from generation to generation through manifest and latent socialization processes.

9. The political security of top conflict-group leaders promotes regulatory efforts on their part.

[118]

10. The presence of conflict-regulating motives, in combination with conciliatory attitudes and the top leaders' political security, constitutes a sufficient explanation for elite conflict-regulating behavior.

11. The structured predominance of elites vis-à-vis nonelites within their own conflict groups is a necessary condition for conflict-regulating outcomes.

12. One or more of four conditions are necessary for structured elite predominance: apolitical quiescence on the part of nonelites; nonelite acquiescent attitudes toward authority; patron-client relations pyramided to the national level; and mass parties with extensive organizational capabilities.

13. Nonelite attributes are not especially helpful in accounting for the nonelite's negative or positive indirect contributions to conflict regulation, nor are they capable of explaining the likelihood that the nonelites will have a direct negative impact. This general proposition emerges from the conclusion that five seemingly plausible nonelite variables cannot account for nonelite behavior. Nonelite attitudes toward conflict-regulating practices, nonelite beliefs and feelings toward the nation, nonelite feelings of being crosspressured, crosscutting divisions at the nonelite level, and segmental isolation are not generally related to conflict-regulating outcomes.

14. Among contemporary nonwestern societies, socio-economic modernization detracts from the likelihood of conflict-regulating outcomes. The modernization process further exacerbates already intense conflicts, promotes nonelite rejection of regulatory practices, and facilitates a violent response.

Each of these fourteen propositions is no more than plausible, although I have greater confidence in the putative validity of some (numbers 1, 2, 3, 7, and 11) than of others (numbers 6, 8, 9, and 13). It is just because they are plausible propositions which might turn out to be valid that additional efforts should be made to try to confirm them, and this despite the recognition that it is a rare proposition indeed which attains validity in political science. Admittedly, the theory as a unified whole will probably not be susceptible to a test in the same handful of societies or by using the same data source. We can, however, test its component hypotheses and their relations to each other as distinct propositions by relying upon different types of evidence and methods.

The distinct hypotheses may be tested in three ways. It

would be most unrealistic to expect quantifiable data to become available for each and every hypothesis. But considering the number of cross-national data banks that are being developed, along with their increasing reliability, it should be possible to test parts of the theory on a quantitative cross-national basis. One particularly relevant data source that is soon to become available is The African National Integration Project.[1] It contains cross-national data on elite and nonelite instability events, attitudes toward "opposing" tribes, demographic variables, modernization levels and rates of change, levels and rates of social mobilization, and so on. I suspect that most cross-national data will have a far greater relevance for nonelite than elite hypotheses, and thus be applicable to the less important "half" of the theory. Yet as was mentioned in the last chapter, a fullscale study of conflict regulation should also include those variables which explain the emergence of intense conflicts when their deleterious consequences continue to be felt after the conflict has become intense. Here cross-national time-series data may be especially relevant.

A second strategy, that of paired comparisons, allows for the inclusion of most of the relevant variables (the cases would be selected partly on this basis and their small number would permit extensive research into these variables), as well as cross-national comparisons capable of testing the hypotheses (the cases would be partly chosen on this basis). Since this study has concentrated upon cases of successful conflict regulation, this method would correct the imbalance by calling for comparisons of successful with unsuccessful cases: Belgium vs. the Spanish Second Republic, Switzerland vs. Ireland circa 1920, Lebanon vs. the Sudan, and Malaysia vs. Nigeria. An excellent model of this method is to be found in a study which relates the appearance of economic innovations to different types of administrative and governmental structures: the hypotheses are tested by paired comparisons of two early industrializers, England and Japan, with two later industrializers, France and China.[2] Rokkan also uses this method in his studies of nation-building patterns and cleavage formation in Western Europe during the last four centuries. This study should be highly relevant in generalizing about the emergence of intense conflicts.[3]

A third method involves the purposeful selection of a case study (or studies) in order to confront the theory with a severe and thus critical test.[4] Michels used this strategy in attempting

[120]

to "prove" that oligarchy is a universal organizational phenomenon. In *Political Parties* he selected the German Social Democratic Party as his focus on the assumption that, if a universal phenomenon, oligarchy should also characterize that political party, even though it claimed to be, and was perhaps universally considered to be, the most democratic in the world. In order to help validate a hypothesis, the case study should be selected so that the hypothesis must survive the test if it is not to be totally or largely invalidated. Here we are relying upon Popper's conception of a valid generalization: a statement which survives purposeful efforts to disprove it. What may be called strategic criteria for the selection of a critical case study vary according to the particular hypotheses being tested.

Several strategic criteria could identify a critical case study for our purposes, though no single case study could validate the entire theory. The first strategic criterion demands extensive variation in the dependent variable; conflict regulation would have had to have failed at one time and succeeded at another. If the theory is not to be disproved the explanatory variables would have had to have been absent in the first and present in the second instance. It should also turn out that the dependent and independent variables had varied concomitantly over time. Austria during the First and Second Republics might qualify as a critical case study, although its acceptability is tarnished by my having partly relied upon the Second Republic experience in developing the hypotheses. A second strategic criterion involves a society which experienced the most intense of intense conflicts, and yet managed to regulate it. A regime which survived this kind of a conflict would presumably require the presence of all our explanatory variables; the absence of one or more of them would sharply call the theory into question. India circa 1960, with its raging linguistic conflict, might serve as a critical case study considering the many writers at the time who predicted the direst consequences for India during "the most dangerous decades." [5] A third type of critical case study would find practically all our explanatory variables present within one segment, absent in the opposing segment, followed by violence or repression. The evidence would then have to show conclusively that regulation failed solely as a result of the behavior of elites and nonelites within that segment in which the explanatory variables were absent.

[121]

Besides efforts to validate it, the theory also needs to be re-fined. In its present form it is almost equally applicable to all deeply divided societies featuring open regimes. This is all right in the initial development of a theory. However, the specificity, explanatory power, and validity of the theory could be increased by differentiating among deeply divided societies according to various criteria. It may be, for example, that some of our hypotheses are more appropriate in accounting for the regulation of intense class conflicts while others can better explain the regulation of intense communal conflicts. If this turns out to be the case, then in a complete theoretical statement such subsidiary propositions should be included. Some hypotheses may be more useful in explaining regulatory outcomes in fully open regimes and less adequate among regimes which are only partly open. It may also be important to distinguish between the regulation of less, but still intense, conflicts and those that are most severe. And, finally, our explanations may vary in their importance according to the type of regulatory failure—whether it be widespread violence, governmental repression, or both. Cross-national quantitative data and the method of paired comparisons could be used both to generate and test such subsidiary hypotheses.

Given the enormous normative significance of violence and repression, both for the individuals living in deeply divided societies and for the political scientists who study them, a fully developed theory should have something to say about strategies and policies which further conflict regulation. The present discussion of regulatory practices does have something to contribute along these lines in suggesting that certain practices are potentially effective, while an exclusive reliance on majoritarian practices and the attempt to create a national identity do not facilitate regulatory outcomes. Yet none of the other hypotheses have a direct policy relevance, nor are the explanatory variables susceptible to manipulation by conflict group leaders or others interested in regulatory outcomes. The only hypothesis that comes even close to satisfying either criterion refers to the presence of well-organized mass parties as one basis of structured elite predominance. It may be that those variables with significant explanatory power are nonmanipulable, and those that are manipulable have little if any explanatory power. Yet, given the singular normative importance of regulatory outcomes, every effort should be made to identify possible variables that are both explanatory and manipulable. Attempts to do so could proceed along two paths. Policy statements might be roughly "deducible" from, or implied by, some of our explanatory variables. It is also possible to think about the problem inductively, beginning with a list of factors that political and governmental leaders are capable of manipulating, and then going on to ascertain whether any of them are capable of contributing to conflict regulation.

In short, it is just because the theory is presumptively valid that it should be tested extensively, refined, and extended to the realm of conflict-regulating policies.

NOTES

INTRODUCTION

1. E. E. Schattschneider, *The Semi-Sovereign People* (New York: Holt, Rinehart, and Winston, 1960), p. 71.
2. An alternative model is currently being explicitly or implicitly developed in some studies of the smaller European democracies cited below.
3. Karl W. Deutsch, *et al.*, *Political Community in the North Atlantic Area* (Princeton: Princeton University Press, 1957).
4. Robert J. Jackson and Michael B. Stein, *Issues in Comparative Politics* (New York: St. Martin's Press, 1971), pp. 116–120. Clifford Geertz's work most closely related to the notion of political integration is "Primordial Sentiments and Civil Politics in the New States," in Clifford Geertz, ed., *Old Societies and New States* (Glencoe: The Free Press, 1963), pp. 102–128.
5. *Same*, pp. 120, 125.
6. Henry Bienen, *Violence and Social Change: A Review of the Current Literature* (Chicago: University of Chicago Press, 1968), p. 90.

CHAPTER I

1. Harry Eckstein, *Division and Cohesion in Democracy: A Study of Norway* (Princeton: Princeton University Press, 1966), pp. 35–36.
2. Ralf Dahrendorf, *Class and Class Conflict in Industrial Society* (Stanford: Stanford University Press, 1959), p. 211.
3. Neil Smelser, *The Theory of Collective Behavior* (New York: The Free Press, 1963).
4. Jürg Steiner, "Nonviolent Conflict Resolution in Democratic Systems: Switzerland," *Journal of Conflict Resolution*, Number 3 (1969), pp. 295–304.
5. Arend Lijphart, The Politics of Accommodation: *Pluralism and Democracy in the Netherlands* (Berkeley: University of California Press, 1968).
6. Donald Rothchild, "Ethnicity and Conflict Resolution," *World Politics*, Number 4 (1970), p. 615.

CHAPTER II

1. Frank A. Pinner, "On the Structure of Organizations and Beliefs: *Lagerdenken* in Austria," (paper delivered at the American Political

Science Meetings, Chicago, 1967), pp. 24–25. Also see Rodney Stiefbold, *Elites and Elections in a Fragmented Political System*, forthcoming.

2. G. Bingham Powell, Jr., *Social Fragmentation and Political Hostility:
An Austrian Case Study* (Stanford: Stanford University Press, 1970),
p. 17.

3. The texts of the coalition pacts are found in Rodney Stiefbold, *et al.*,
eds., *Wahlen und Parteien in Österreich* (Vienna: Verlag für Jugend
und Volk, 1966), Volume B, pp. 779–785.

4. Jürg Steiner, "The Principles of Majority and Proportionality," *British
Journal of Political Science*, Number 1 (January 1971), p. 63.

5. Michael C. Hudson, "Democracy and Social Mobilization in Lebanese
Politics," *Comparative Politics*, Number 2 (January 1969), pp. 249–
258.

9. Michael C. Hudson, *The Precarious Republic: Modernization in Lebanon* (New York: Random House, 1968), p. 23.

7. Pierre Rondot, "The Political Institutions of Lebanese Democracy,"
in Leonard Binder, ed., *Politics in Lebanon* (New York: John Wiley,
1966), p. 129.

8. Iliya F. Harik, "The Ethnic Revolution in the Middle East," (paper
delivered at the American Political Science Association Meetings,
New York, 1969), p. 13; Michael W. Suleiman, "Elections in a Confessional Democracy," *Journal of Politics*, Number 2 (1967), p. 111.

9. Lode Claes, "The Process of Federalization in Belgium," *Delta*, Number 4 (Winter, 1963–64), p. 46.

10. *Same.*

11. Herbert P. Secher, "Coalition Government: The Case of the Second
Austrian Republic," *American Political Science Review*, 52 (September
1958), pp. 799 ff.

12. John C. Calhoun, *A Disquisition on Government* (New York: The Liberal Arts Press, 1953), p. 52.

13. *Same*, pp. 52–53.

14. Frederick C. Engelmann, "Austria: The Pooling of Opposition," in
Robert A. Dahl, ed., *Political Oppositions in Western Democracies*
(New Haven: Yale University Press, 1966), p. 266; Secher, "Coali-
tion Government. . . ," p. 797.

15. Claes, "The Process. . . ," p. 45.

16. Private communication from Michael C. Hudson, July 20, 1971.

17. Binder, ed., *Politics in Lebanon*, pp. 9, 190, 288; Suleiman, "Elections. . . ," pp. 116, 225.

18. Milton J. Esman, *Administration and Development in Malaysia: In-
stitution Building and Reform in a Plural Society* (Ithaca: Cornell
University Press, forthcoming 1972), Chapter VII.

19. For a basic typology of compromise formulas, see Dankwart A. Rustow,
*The Politics of Compromise: A Study of Parties and Cabinet Govern-
ment in Sweden* (Princeton: Princeton University Press, 1955), pp.
231–232.

20. Gerhard Lehmbruch, "A Non-Competitive Pattern of Conflict Management in Liberal Democracies: The Case of Switzerland, Austria and

Lebanon," (paper delivered at the International Political Science Association Meetings, Brussels, 1967), p. 3.

21. Hans Daalder, "The Netherlands: Opposition in a Segmented Society," in Dahl, ed., *Political Oppositions. . .* , pp. 205, 222; Lijphart, *The Politics of. . .* , pp. 103–112.
22. Val R. Lorwin, "Belgium: Religion, Class and Language in National Politics," in Dahl, ed., *Political Oppositions. . .* , p. 150.
23. *Same*, pp. 169–170.
24. Esman, *Administration and Development. . .* , Chapter II.
25. Crane Brinton, *The Anatomy of Revolution* (New York: Random House, 1957), p. 39.
26. Alexis de Tocqueville, *The Old Regime and the French Revolution* (New York: Doubleday, 1955), p. 177.
27. Félix Bonjour, *et al.*, *A Short History of Switzerland* (London: Oxford University Press, 1966), pp. 272 and *passim*; Hans Kohn, *Nationalism and Liberty: The Swiss Example* (New York: Macmillan, 1956), pp. 106–112.
28. Ali A. Mazrui, "Pluralism and National Integration," in Leo Kuper and M. G. Smith, eds., *Pluralism in Africa* (Berkeley: University of California Press, 1969), p. 338.
29. Donald Rothchild, "The Limits of Federalism: An Examination of Political Institutional Transfer in Africa," *Journal of Modern African Studies*, Number 3 (November 1966), p. 276.
30. Robert A. Dahl, "Some Explanations," in Dahl, ed., *Political Oppositions. . .* , p. 357.
31. Similar conclusions would also emerge if the six practices were compared with Gerhard Lehmbruch, *Proporzdemokratie* (Tübingen: J. C. B. Mohr, 1967), pp. 43–47.
32. Dahl, *Political Oppositions. . .* , p. 357.
33. Calhoun, *A Disquisition. . .* , p. 29.
34. *Same*, p. 33.
35. Lehmbruch, "A Non-Competitive. . . ," pp. 2–3.
36. W. G. Runciman, "Charismatic Legitimacy and One-Party Rule in Ghana," *Archives europeènes de sociologie*, Number 1 (1963), pp. 149–151.
37. Rupert Emerson, "Parties and National Integration in Africa," in Joseph LaPalombara and Myron Weiner, eds., *Political Parties and Political Development* (Princeton: Princeton University Press, 1966), pp. 278–281; David E. Apter, "Ghana," in James S. Coleman and Carl G. Rosberg, eds., *Political Parties and National Integration in Tropical Africa* (Berkeley: University of California Press, 1964), pp. 295–300.
38. Emerson, "Parties and National Integration. . . ," p. 278.
39. McKim Marriott, "Cultural Policy in the New States," in Geertz, ed., *Old Societies and New States*, p. 42.
40. Geertz, *same*, p. 123; see also, W. Howard Wriggins, "Impediments to Unity in New Nations: The Case of Ceylon," *American Political Science Review*, 55 (June 1961), pp. 316, 319.
41. William T. Bluhm, "Nation Building: The Case of Austria," *Polity*, Number 2 (Winter 1968), p. 163. We might also note that one mild

effort was made to create a national identity during the First Austrian Republic. And in accordance with our previous generalizations, even though the effort was based upon the application of traditional ideas, it exacerbated rather than mitigated conflicts, and the "Austrian idea" featured authoritarian control and governmental repression. *Same*, p. 151.

42. Leonard Binder, "Political Change in Lebanon," in Binder, ed., *Politics in Lebanon*, pp. 284, 286, 288.

CHAPTER III

1. R. A. Schermerhorn, *Comparative Ethnic Relations: A Framework for Theory and Research* (New York: Random House, 1970), p. 24.

2. In addition, we shall focus upon elite motives because — in spite of their importance—students of comparative politics have paid little attention to them. Elites are generally discussed in terms of social backgrounds, recruitment and career patterns, and role perceptions, with only passing reference to motives. Although this is not necessarily the better strategy for arriving at empirical generalizations, political scientists have preferred the company of Talcott Parsons' actors who rely upon attitudes and role definitions in orienting themselves toward action without ever actually acting, to the historians' unique but generalizable political actors who need no such analytic prodding to get them to act. It is perhaps just this neglect of motivations which helps account for one political scientist's lament that "elite behavior seems to be more elusive and less susceptible to empirical generalization than mass phenomena." [Arend Lijphart, "Typologies of Democratic Systems," *Comparative Political Studies*, Number 1 (1968), p. 25.] Given the political self-awareness and goal-oriented behavior of elites compared to nonelites, omitting their motivations will weaken any empirical generalization.

3. Georg Simmel, *Conflict* (New York: The Free Press, 1955), p. 103, emphasis in the original.

4. Val R. Lorwin, "Segmented Pluralism: Ideological Cleavages and Political Cohesion in the Smaller European Democracies," *Comparative Politics*, Number 2 (January 1971), p. 150.

5. Hassan Saab, "The Rationalist School in Lebanese Politics," in Binder, ed., *Politics in Lebanon*, p. 276; Albert Hourani, "Lebanon: The Development of a Political Society," in *same*, pp. 27–28.

6. Pinner, "On the Structure. . . ," p. 11; Walter Goldinger, *Geschichte der Republik Österreich* (Vienna: Verlag für Geschichte und Politik, 1962), p. 286; Frederick C. Engelmann, "Haggling for the Equilibrium: The Renegotiation of the Austrian Coalition, 1959," *American Political Science Review*, 54 (1962), p. 653.

7. Lorwin, "Belgium. . . ," p. 154.

8. Lijphart, *The Politics of*. . . , pp. 110–111.

9. Bonjour, *et al.*, *A Short History*. . . , pp. 261 ff; and William E. Rappard, *Collective Security in Swiss Experience: 1291–1948* (London: Allen and Unwin, 1948), pp. 64 and *passim*.

10. Lorwin, "Belgium. . . ," p. 151.
11. Carl Landauer, *European Socialism* (Berkeley: University of California Press, 1959), Vol. I, p. 476.
12. André Philippart, "Belgium: Language and Class Oppositions," *Government and Opposition*, Number 1 (November 1966), p. 69.
13. Bonjour, *et al.*, *A Short History*. . . , pp. 270–272.
14. Rodney Stiefbold, "Segmented Pluralism and Constitutional Democracy in Austria," in Norman Vig and Rodney Stiefbold, eds., *Politics in Advanced Nations* (New York: Appleton-Century-Crofts, forthcoming).
15. R. S. Milne and K. J. Ratnam, "Politics and Finance in Malaya," *Journal of Commonwealth Studies*, Number 3 (1965), pp. 192 ff.
16. Landauer, *European Socialism*, p. 467.
17. Jean Meynaud, *et al.*, *La Décision politique* (Paris: Cahiers de la Fondation des Sciences Politiques, 1965), pp. 159 and *passim*.
18. George Armstrong Kelly, "Biculturalism and Party Systems in Belgium and Canada," in John D. Montgomery and Albert O. Hirschman, eds., *Public Policy* (Cambridge, Mass.: Harvard University Press, 1967), p. 353; Philippart, "Belgium. . . ," p. 70.
19. Lijphart, *The Politics of*. . . , pp. 110–111.
20. Bonjour, *et al.*, *A Short History*. . . , p. 258. It has also been claimed that these same Protestant Radicals were motivated to make concessions and compromises to the Catholics during the twenty years after the brief civil war in order to avoid Protestant suffering if strife were to be renewed. [Steiner, "Nonviolent Conflict Resolution. . . ," p. 302.] However, this claim is somewhat implausible since violence was highly unlikely after 1848. The Protestants had won a clear-cut military victory and the Catholics were mollified by the concessions granted them.
21. Engelmann, "Haggling for. . . ," p. 652; U. W. Kitzinger, "Wahlkampf in Österreich," in Stiefbold, *et al.*, eds., *Wahlen und Parteien*. . . , Vol. B. p. 445; Stiefbold, "Segmented Pluralism," in Vig and Stiefbold, *Politics*. . .
22. Hudson, *The Precarious Republic*, pp. 249–258.
23. *The Economist* (London, May 17, 1969).
24. Esman, *Administration and Development*. . . , Chapter VII.

CHAPTER IV

1. Hans Daalder, "On Building Consociational Nations," (paper delivered at UNESCO Meeting on the Problems of State Formation and National Building, Cerisy-la-Salle, 1970), p. 16.
2. Dahl, *Political Oppositions*. . . , p. 354.
3. Eric A. Nordlinger, *The Working Class Tories: Authority, Deference and Stable Democracy* (Berkeley: University of California Press, 1967), pp. 51–55.
4. Seymour Martin Lipset, *et al.*, *Union Democracy* (New York: Doubleday, 1962), p. 16; Daalder, "The Netherlands. . . ," p. 216; Lijphart, *The Politics of*. . . , p. 193.

5. Neal E. Miller and John Dollard, *Social Learning and Imitation* (New Haven: Yale University Press, 1941); B. F. Skinner, *Science and Human Behavior* (New York: Macmillan, 1953); George C. Homans, *Social Behavior: Its Elementary Forms* (London: Routledge and Kegan Paul, 1961).

6. Daalder, "On Building. . . ," pp. 3–4.

7. *Same*, pp. 4, 6, 7.

8. *Same*, pp. 7, 8.

9. Steiner, "The Principles of. . . ," p. 67.

10. G. J. Renier, *The Dutch Nation: An Historical Study* (London: Allen and Unwin, 1944), pp. 35–36, 51.

11. Daalder, "The Netherlands. . . ," p. 193.

12. Daalder, "On Building. . . ," pp. 3, 18.

13. Steiner, "The Principles of. . . ," p. 67.

14. Daalder, "On Building. . . ," *passim.*

15. Lorwin, "Segmented Pluralism. . . ," p. 160; Charles A. Gulick, *Austria from Hapsburg to Hitler* (Berkeley: University of California Press, 1948), Vol. I, p. 694; Alfred Diamant, *Austrian Catholics and the First Republic* (Princeton: Princeton University Press, 1960), pp. 103, 149 and *passim.*

16. For an analysis of the Ecumenical Councils, showing how situational threats to Church authority are related to punitiveness, dogmatism, and closed-mindedness, see Milton Rokeach, *The Open and Closed Mind* (New York: Basic Books, 1960), pp. 376–388.

17. I am not aware of any studies which touch upon these socio-psychological hypotheses in the case of deeply divided societies. However, two studies—one of an American governmental agency and the other of Burmese bureaucrats—indirectly support the hypotheses. Insecurities are said to be related to mutual distrust, individual isolation, a rigid adherence to established practices, and a reliance upon the safest course of action rather than trial-and-error activities. See Peter M. Blau, *The Dynamics of Bureaucracy* (Chicago: University of Chicago Press, 1955), p. 208; Lucian Pye, *Politics, Personality and Nation-Building* (New Haven: Yale University Press, 1962), p. 228.

18. Lijphart, "Typologies. . . ," pp. 20–23; Arend Lijphart, "Consociational Democracy," *World Politics*, 21 (January 1969), p. 216.

19. Lijphart, "Typologies. . . ," pp. 17, 20.

20. *Same*, pp. 22–23.

21. Esman, *Administration and Development*, Chapter II.

22. Lijphart, "Typologies. . . ," p. 23.

23. *Same*.

24. *Same*.

CHAPTER V

1. Dahrendorf, *Class and Class Conflict. . .* , pp. 226, 259.

2. The hypothesis is supported by a number of studies which argue that democratic stability is related to greater consensus among elites than within the nonelite. The relevant studies are cited and the hypothesis

tested in Ian Budge, *Democratic Argument and Democratic Stability* (Chicago: Markham, 1970).

3. Frantz Fanon, *The Wretched of the Earth* (New York: Grove Press, 1966), p. 107.
4. James L. Payne, *Patterns of Conflict in Colombia* (New Haven: Yale University Press, 1968), pp. 159–177; Robert H. Dix, *Colombia: The Political Dimensions of Change* (New Haven: Yale University Press, 1967), pp. 360–369.
5. While Colombia is obviously not a case of successful conflict regulation, it is worth noting that when the military dictator (Rojas Pinilla) was overthrown in 1957, the party leaders worked out a sophisticated regulatory practice of the proportionality type. Each party was to be allotted 50 per cent of the legislative seats and the powerful presidency was to rotate every four years (for sixteen years) between Liberals and Conservatives. The great bulk of positions in the civil service and government-owned corporations was to be filled on a parity basis. Given the fifty-fifty division of legislative seats a fourth aspect of the regulatory agreement constituted a mutual veto: the Congress could only pass legislation by a two-thirds vote. See Dix, *Colombia. . . ,* pp. 133–134.
6. Donald L. Horowitz, "Multiracial Politics in the New States: Toward a Theory of Conflict," in Jackson and Stein, *Issues. . . ,* pp. 168–169; Robert H. Kearney, *Communalism and Language in the Politics of Ceylon* (Durham: Duke University Press, 1967), pp. 85 and *passim.*
7. Ernst Nolte, *Three Faces of Fascism* (New York: Holt, Rinehart and Winston, 1966), pp. 196–208.
8. *Same,* p. 206.
9. Erich Grüner, *Die Parteien in der Schweitz* (Bern: Franche Verlag, 1969), pp. 50–54.
10. Esman, *Administration and Development. . . ,* Chapter II.
11. *Same.* For example, the 1957 Constitution called for the reconsideration of the language issue in ten years. In 1967 the conflict group leaders hammered out an agreement which included only the minimal demands of their respective followers. Acquiescent attitudes did not constrain rumblings of protest from the Chinese, nor did they prevent Malay university students and school teachers from challenging their leaders' compromise through marches and demonstrations, and many other Malays from joining a National Language Front to assail the Malay leaders. Yet both elites were able to hold firm against the demands of the extremists (even when they mobilized substantial rank-and-file support), to calm their followers, attain their questioning approval, and enact the language bill. Admittedly, since 1969 nonelites have been less deferential to their traditional leaders, but alternative attitudes, leaders or procedures have not yet appeared.
12. Jean Grossholtz, "Integrative Factors in the Malaysian and Philippine Legislatures," *Comparative Politics,* 3 (October 1970), p. 107.
13. Lijphart, *The Politics of. . . ,* pp. 144–162, 207.
14. *Same,* p. 111.
15. Eric Wolf, "Aspects of Group Relations in a Complex Society: Mexico,"

in Dwight Heath and Richard Adams, eds., *Contemporary Cultures and Societies of Latin America* (New York: Random House, 1965), p. 97.
16. Hudson, *The Precarious Republic. . . ,* p. 19.
17. Arnold Hottinger, "Zu'ama' in Historical Perspective," in Binder, ed., *Politics in Lebanon,* pp. 85–89, 91.
18. Hudson, *The Precarious Republic. . . ,* p. 92. In a private communication to the writer Hudson indicated that the Lebanese nonelite also tends to conform to the conditions of apolitical quiescence and acquiescence.
19. Pinner, "On the Structure. . . ," p. 14.
20. Peter Pulzer, "The Legitimizing Role of Political Parties: The Second Austrian Republic," *Government and Opposition,* Number 3 (Summer 1969), p. 337.
21. Pinner, "On the Structure. . . ," p. 15.
22. *Same.*
23. Powell, *Social Fragmentation. . . ,* pp. 52–54. It is therefore not surprising to find an analysis of 1965–1966 survey data indicating that 60 per cent of the population is securely integrated into either the Socialist or People's Party subculture. See K. Liepelt, "Esquisse d'une typologie des electeurs allemans et autrichiens," *Revue française de sociologie,* (janvier-mars, 1968), pp. 16, 23.
24. Val R. Lorwin, "Labor Organizations and Politics in Belgium and France," in Everett Kassolow, ed., *National Labor Movements in the Post-War World* (Pittsburgh: University of Pittsburgh Press, 1963), p. 165.
25. Aristide R. Zolberg, "Political Development in Belgium: Crises and Process," to appear in a volume edited by Raymond Grew on the crises of political development in Europe.
26. Landauer, *European Socialism,* pp. 476 ff.
27. Lorwin, "Labor Organizations. . . ," pp. 143–144, 159.
28. Cited in Lorwin, "Segmented Pluralism. . . ," p. 156.
29. That part of the hypothesis referring to the four conditions of structured elite predominance, might just hold in all open regimes, whether an intense conflict is or is not raging. There is little in the hypothesis that makes it especially applicable to deeply divided societies.

CHAPTER VI

1. Lijphart, "Typologies. . . ," p. 28; Lijphart, "Consociational Democracy," pp. 213–214.
2. Lijphart, "Typologies. . . ," p. 28, italics in the original.
3. *Same.*
4. Bluhm, "Nation Building. . . ," p. 159.
5. *Same,* pp. 158–160.
6. Lijphart, "Typologies. . . ," pp. 29–30.
7. *Same,* p. 29, citing Lorwin, "Belgium. . . ," p. 176; and Stiefbold *et al.,* eds., *Wahlen und Parteien,* Vol. B, pp. 584–558.
8. The proposition has been developed, or its validity attested to by such

highly respected writers as Bentley, Truman, Kornhauser, Lipset, Key, Parsons, Deutsch, Lane, Coser, Almond, Rokkan and Huntington, among others.

9. Lewis A. Coser, *The Functions of Social Conflict* (New York: The Free Press, 1956), pp. 72 and *passim.*
10. Seymour Martin Lipset, *Political Man* (Garden City: Doubleday, 1958), pp. 31, 88–89. Elsewhere the connection with stable democracy is advanced as a tendency statement rather than as a necessary condition.
11. Bernard Berelson, *et al.*, *Voting* (Chicago: University of Chicago Press, 1954), pp. 128 ff.; Angus Campbell, *et al.*, *The American Voter* (New York: John Wiley, 1960), pp. 77–88; V. O. Key, *Public Opinion and American Democracy* (New York: Knopf, 1961), p. 69.
12. Sidney Verba, "Organizational Membership and Democratic Consensus," *Journal of Politics*, 27 (May 1965), pp. 465–508.
13. Powell, *Social Fragmentation.* . . , pp. 37–38.
14. Philip E. Converse, "The Nature of Belief Systems in Mass Politics," in David E. Apter, ed., *Ideology and Discontent* (New York: The Free Press, 1964), Chapter 6; Herbert McCloskey, *et al.*, "Issue Conflict and Consensus Among Party Leaders and Followers," *American Political Science Review*, 54 (June 1960), pp. 406–427; Key, *Public Opinion*, pp. 152–181.
15. Robert Melson and Howard Wolpe, "Modernization and the Politics of Communalism: A Theoretical Perspective," *American Political Science Review*, Number 4 (December 1970), p. 1127.
16. *Same.*
17. *Same*, pp. 1127–1128.
18. Richard Rose, *Governing without Consensus: An Irish Perspective* (Boston: Beacon Press, 1971), p. 359.
19. Esman, *Administration and Development.* . . , Chapter II.
20. Fred Anderson, *et al.*, *Issues in Political Development* (Englewood Cliffs, N.J.: Prentice-Hall, 1967), p. 26.
21. *Same*, pp. 26–27.
22. Lorwin, "Belgium. . . ," p. 178.
23. Stiefbold, *Elites and.* . . , Chapter V.
24. Rose, *Governing without Consensus*, p. 388.
25. Dahl, *Political Oppositions.* . . , p. 378, italics in the original.
26. Lijphart, "Typologies. . . ," p. 25.
27. *Same*; Lijphart, *The Politics of.* . . , p. 198.
28. Lijphart, "Typologies. . . ," p. 26.
29. *Same*, p. 25; Lijphart, *The Politics of.* . . , pp. 200–202.
30. Esman, *Administration and Development.* . . , Chapter VII.
31. Lorwin, "Segmental Pluralism. . . ," p. 165. Also see Arnold J. Heidenheimer, "Elite Responses to *Ontzuiling*: Reels within Wheels in Dutch Broadcasting Politics," (paper presented at the Eighth World Congress of Political Science, Munich, 1970).
32. Rose, *Governing without Consensus*, pp. 308–309.
33. Melson and Wolpe, "Modernization. . . ," p. 1119.
34. Here we might take note of the claim that "minorities which are

territorially concentrated do not compromise as easily as those which are fairly evenly dispersed." K. J. Ratnam, *Communalism and the Political Process in Malaya* (Kuala Lumpur: University of Malaya Press, 1965), p. 210.

35. J. S. Furnivall, *Colonial Policy and Practice* (Cambridge: Cambridge University Press, 1948),

36. M. G. Smith, *The Plural Society in the British West Indies* (Berkeley: University of California Press, 1965), esp. pp. xi–xiii; M. G. Smith, "Institutional and Political Conditions of Pluralism," in Kuper and Smith, *Pluralism in Africa*, p. 27; Horowitz, in Jackson and Stein, *Issues. . .* , pp. 164–166.

37. Eric A. Nordlinger, "Political Development: Time Sequences and Rates of Change," *World Politics*, 20 (April 1968), pp. 514–519.

CHAPTER VII

1. M. Mitchell, *et al.*, *Black Africa: A Handbook for Comparative Analysis* (New York: The Free Press, forthcoming).

2. Robert Holt and John Turner, *The Political Basis of Economic Development* (Princeton: Van Nostrand, 1966).

3. Stein Rokkan, "The Structuring of Mass Politics in the Smaller European Democracies: A Developmental Typology," *Comparative Studies in Society and History*, 10 (January 1968), pp. 179–210; and "The Growth and Structuring of Mass Politics in Western Europe: Reflections on Possible Models of Explanation," *Scandinavian Political Studies*, 5 (1970), pp. 65–84.

4. For a persuasive attempt to redress the imbalance between case studies and cross-national studies in the development and testing of hypotheses, see Harry Eckstein, "Case Study and Theory in Macropolitics," Princeton University, mimeograph, 1971.

5. For example, see Selig Harrison, *India: The Most Dangerous Decades* (Princeton: Princeton University Press, 1958).

RECENT BOOKS WRITTEN UNDER THE CENTER'S AUSPICES *

Taxation and Development: Lessons from Colombian Experience, by Richard M. Bird, 1969. Harvard University Press. ISBN 0–674–86840–4.

Students in Revolt, ed. Seymour M. Lipset and Philip G. Altbach, 1969. Houghton Mifflin.

The Process of Modernization: An Annotated Bibliography on the Sociocultural Aspects of Development, by John Brode, 1969. Harvard University Press. ISBN 0–674–71070–3.

Protest and Power in Black Africa, eds. Robert I. Rotberg and Ali A. Mazrui, 1970. Oxford University Press.

Agricultural Development in India's Districts: The Intensive Agricultural Districts Programme, by Dorris D. Brown, 1970. Harvard University Press. SBN 674–01230–5.

Authoritarian Politics in Modern Society: The Dynamics of Established One-Party Systems, eds. Samuel P. Huntington and Clement H. Moore, 1970. Basic Books. ISBN 0–465–00569–1.

Europe's Would-Be Polity, by Leon Lindberg and Stuart A. Scheingold, 1970. Prentice-Hall.

Lord and Peasant in Peru, by F. LaMond Tullis, 1970. Harvard University Press. ISBN 0–674–53914–1.

Peace in Europe, by Karl E. Birnbaum, 1970. Oxford University Press. ISBN 0–19–2850423.

The Logic of Images in International Relations, by Robert Jervis, 1970. Princeton University Press. 07532–8.

Korean Development: The Interplay of Politics and Economics, by David C. Cole and Princeton N. Lyman, 1971. Harvard University Press. SBN 674–50563–8.

Nuclear Diplomacy, by George H. Quester, 1971. The Dunellen Co., Inc.

Political Mobilization of the Venezuelan Peasant, by John D. Powell, 1971. Harvard University Press. ISBN 0–674–68626–8.

The Kennedy Round in American Trade Policy, by John W. Evans, 1971. Harvard University Press.

Peace in Parts: Integration and Conflict in Regional Organization, by Joseph S. Nye, 1971. Little, Brown and Co.

International Norms and War between States: Three Studies in International Politics, by Kjell Goldmann, 1971. Published in cooperation between *Läromedelsförlagen* (Sweden) and the Swedish Institute of International Affairs.

Studies in Development Planning, ed. Hollis B. Chenery, 1971. Harvard University Press.

* A full list of titles may be obtained from the Publications Office at the CFIA.

Higher Education in a Transitional Society: A Study of the University of Bombay, by Philip G. Altbach, 1971. Sindhu Publications (Bombay).

Higher Education in India, eds. Amrik Singh and Philip G. Altbach, 1971. Oxford University Press (Delhi).

Development Policy II: The Pakistan Experience, eds. Walter P. Falcon and Gustav F. Papanek, 1971. Harvard University Press.

Transnational Relations and World Politics, eds. Joseph S. Nye and Robert O. Keohane, forthcoming from Harvard University Press. Also published in *International Organization* (Summer 1971).

Sovereignty at Bay: The Multinational Spread of U.S. Enterprise, by Raymond Vernon, 1971. Basic Books.

Passion and Politics: Student Activism in America, by S. M. Lipset with Gerald Schäflander, 1971. Little, Brown and Co.

FORTHCOMING PUBLICATIONS

Latin American University Students: A Six Nation Comparative Study, by Arthur Liebman *et al.*, forthcoming April 1972 from Harvard University Press.

The Myth of the Guerrilla, by J. Bowyer Bell, forthcoming from Blond (London) and Knopf (New York).

Peasants against Politics: Rural Organization in Brittany, 1911–1967, by Suzanne Berger, forthcoming from Harvard University Press.

The Politics of Land Reform in Chile, 1950–1970, by Robert R. Kaufman, forthcoming from Harvard University Press.

The Politics of Nonviolent Action, by Gene E. Sharp, forthcoming from The Pilgrim Press.

Becoming Modern, by Alex Inkeles, forthcoming from Little, Brown and Co.

The International Politics of African Boundaries, by Saadia Touval, forthcoming from Harvard University Press.

OCCASIONAL PAPERS IN INTERNATIONAL AFFAIRS

1. *A Plan for Planning: The Need for a Better Method of Assisting Under-developed Countries on Their Economic Policies*, by Gustav F. Papanek, 1961. Out of print.*
2. *The Flow of Resources from Rich to Poor*, by Alan D. Neale, 1961. Out of print.*
3. *Limited War: An Essay on the Development of the Theory and an Annotated Bibliography*, by Morton H. Halperin, 1962. Out of print.*
4. *Reflections on the Failure of the First West Indian Federation*, by Hugh W. Springer, 1962. Out of print.*
5. *On the Interaction of Opposing Forces under Possible Arms Agreements*, by Glenn A. Kent, 1963. 36 pp. $1. ISBN 0–87674–001–8.
6. *Europe's Northern Cap and the Soviet Union*, by Nils Örvik, 1963. Out of print.*
7. *Civil Administration in the Punjab: An Analysis of a State Government in India*, by E. N. Mangat Rai, 1963. 82 pp. $1. ISBN 0–87674–003–2.
8. *On the Appropriate Size of a Development Program*, by Edward S. Mason, 1964. 24 pp. 75 cents. ISBN 0–87674–004–2.
9. *Self-Determination Revisited in the Era of Decolonization*, by Rupert Emerson, 1964. 64 pp. $1.25. ISBN 0–87674–005–0.
10. *The Planning and Execution of Economic Development in Southeast Asia*, by Clair Wilcox, 1965. 27 pp. $1. ISBN 0–87674–006–9.
11. *Pan-Africanism in Action*, by Albert Tevoedjre, 1965. 88 pp. $2. ISBN 0–87674–007–7.
12. *Is China Turning In?* by Morton H. Halperin, 1965. 34 pp. $1. ISBN 0–87674–008–5.
13. *Economic Development in India and Pakistan*, by Edward S. Mason, 1966. Out of print.*
14. *The Role of the Military in Recent Turkish Politics*, by Ergun Özbudun, 1966. 54 pp. $1.25. ISBN 0–87674–009–3.
15. *Economic Development and Individual Change: A Social-Psychological Study of the Comilla Experiment in Pakistan*, by Howard Schuman, 1967. Out of print.*
16. *A Select Bibliography on Students, Politics, and Higher Education*, by Philip G. Altbach, UMHE Revised Edition, 1970. 65 pp. $2.50. ISBN 0–87674–011–5.
17. *Europe's Political Puzzle: A Study of the Fouchet Negotiations and the 1963 Veto*, by Alessandro Silj, 1967. 178 pp. $2.50. ISBN 0–87674–012–3.
18. *The Cap and the Straits: Problems of Nordic Security*, by Jan Klenberg, 1968. 19 pp. $1. ISBN 0–87674–013–1.

* Out-of-print titles may be ordered from AMS Press, Inc., 56 East 13th Street, New York City, N.Y. 10003.

19. *Cyprus: The Law and Politics of Civil Strife,* by Linda B. Miller, 1968. 97 pp. $2.50. ISBN 0–87674–014–X.
20. *East and West Pakistan: A Problem in the Political Economy of Regional Planning,* by Md. Anisur Rahman, 1968. Out of print.*
21. *Internal War and International Systems: Perspectives on Method,* by George A. Kelly and Linda B. Miller, 1969. 40 pp. $2. ISBN 0–87674–016–6.
22. *Migrants, Urban Poverty, and Instability in Developing Nations,* by Joan M. Nelson, 1969. 83 pp. $2.25. ISBN 0–87674–017–4.
23. *Growth and Development in Pakistan, 1955–1969,* by Joseph J. Stern and Walter P. Falcon, 1970. 94 pp. $2.75. ISBN 0–87674–018–2.
24. *Higher Education in Developing Countries: A Bibliography,* by Philip G. Altbach, 1970. 118 pp. $3.75. ISBN 0–87674–019–0.
25. *Anatomy of Political Institutionalization: The Case of Israel and Some Comparative Analyses,* by Amos Perlmutter, 1970. 60 pp. $2.25. ISBN 0–87674–020–4.
26. *The German Democratic Republic from the Sixties to the Seventies,* by Peter C. Ludz, 1970. 100 pp. $3.00. ISBN 0–87674–021–2.
27. *The Law in Political Integration: The Evolution and Integrative Implications of Regional Legal Processes in the European Community,* by Stuart A. Scheingold, 1971. 63 pp. $2.25. ISBN 0–87674–022–0.
28. *Psychological Dimensions of U.S.-Japanese Relations,* by Hiroshi Kitamura, 1971. 45 pp. $1.75. ISBN 0–87674–023–9.
29. *Conflict Regulation in Divided Societies,* by Eric A. Nordlinger, 1972. 137 pp. $4.00. ISBN 0–87674–024–7.